The Hidden Power of Oaths
Invisible Pacts That Rule Your Life

How to Identify, Release, and Heal the Unconscious
Agreements That Limit Your Life

Alan Bradley

Original Title:
The Hidden Power of Oaths
Copyright © 2025, published by Luiz Antonio dos Santos ME.
This book is a non-fiction work that explores practices and concepts in the field of personal development and spirituality. Through a comprehensive approach, the author offers practical tools to achieve emotional balance, prosperity, and personal fulfillment.

1st Edition

Production Team
Author: Alan Bradley
Editor: Luiz Santos
Cover: Studios Booklas / Théo Damaris
Consultant: Caio Rennar
Researchers: M. Távora / Jan Brelow / Solange Ferrick
Layout Design: Elisa Varnel

Publication and Identification
The Hidden Power of Oaths
Booklas, 2025
Categories: Personal Development / Spirituality / Holism
DDC: 158.1 — CDU: 159.923.2
All rights reserved to:
Luiz Antonio dos Santos ME / Booklas
No part of this book may be reproduced, stored in a retrieval system, or transmitted by any means — electronic, mechanical, photocopying, recording, or otherwise — without prior and express permission from the copyright holder.

Summary

Systematic Index 5
Prologue 10
Chapter 1 Desperate Cry 13
Chapter 2 Pacts and Vows 19
Chapter 3 The Power of the Word 26
Chapter 4 Spiritual Bargaining 32
Chapter 5 Invisible Bonds 39
Chapter 6 Past Lives 45
Chapter 7 The Law of Karma 50
Chapter 8 Broken Word 56
Chapter 9 Subtle Consequences 61
Chapter 10 Guilt and Fear 66
Chapter 11 Spiritual Entities 71
Chapter 12 Subtle Energies 77
Chapter 13 Spiritual Contracts 83
Chapter 14 Hidden Influence 89
Chapter 15 Repetitive Patterns 95
Chapter 16 Self-Sabotage 101
Chapter 17 Emotional Blockages 107
Chapter 18 Life Limitations 113
Chapter 19 The Shadow of the Past 119
Chapter 20 Signs of the Pact 124
Chapter 21 Spiritual Memory 130

Chapter 22 Inherited Bonds 136
Chapter 23 Retrieving the Past 142
Chapter 24 Spiritual Autonomy 148
Chapter 25 Free Decision 154
Chapter 26 Breaking Ties 160
Chapter 27 Symbolic Ritual 166
Chapter 28 Forgiveness and Release 171
Chapter 29 Spiritual Protection 177
Chapter 30 Self-Transformation 183
Chapter 31 Spiritual Freedom 189
Chapter 32 The Path Ahead 194
Epilogue 200

Systematic Index

Chapter 1: Desperate Cry - This chapter addresses how, in moments of extreme helplessness and despair, humans often make primal promises and pacts to higher forces in exchange for salvation.

Chapter 2: Pacts and Vows - This chapter details the different forms of commitment—promises, oaths, vows, and pacts—and their energetic weight and ability to shape reality.

Chapter 3: The Power of the Word - This chapter explores how spoken words, especially when charged with intention and emotion, become vehicles of creative energy that program one's energetic system and influence reality.

Chapter 4: Spiritual Bargaining - This chapter discusses the human impulse to negotiate with divine or cosmic forces in moments of crisis, offering commitments in exchange for intervention.

Chapter 5: Invisible Bonds - This chapter describes how pacts and vows create persistent, invisible energetic bonds that can influence an individual's life regardless of conscious memory.

Chapter 6: Past Lives - This chapter introduces the concept that energetic commitments made in previous incarnations can continue to influence the present life through the soul's deep memory.

Chapter 7: The Law of Karma - This chapter explains how the karmic law of cause and effect applies to vows and pacts, ensuring that every commitment generates corresponding consequences and lessons.

Chapter 8: Broken Word - This chapter examines the energetic and karmic consequences of breaking sacred commitments, including internal misalignment and the creation of spiritual debt.

Chapter 9: Subtle Consequences - This chapter delves into the deeper, often hidden effects of broken commitments, such as energetic blockages, thought-forms, and environmental imprints.

Chapter 10: Guilt and Fear - This chapter explores how guilt and fear often arise as emotional guardians of unresolved pacts, binding individuals to the past and hindering liberation.

Chapter 11: Spiritual Entities - This chapter discusses how pacts can involve non-corporeal beings, ranging from benevolent guides to self-serving entities, and the varying dynamics and consequences of such agreements.

Chapter 12: Subtle Energies - This chapter broadens the scope of pacts to include commitments made to abstract forces, elevated principles, or collective energy fields (egregores) that can exert binding influence.

Chapter 13: Spiritual Contracts - This chapter introduces the idea that individual pacts and vows can be understood as clauses within larger pre-incarnational soul contracts, shaping life's challenges for evolutionary purposes.

Chapter 14: Hidden Influence - This chapter details how ancient soul agreements and pacts subtly yet tenaciously shape daily choices, emotions, and circumstances, often without conscious awareness.

Chapter 15: Repetitive Patterns - This chapter explains how the unresolved energy of ancient commitments manifests as stubborn, recurring cycles of events, relationships, and obstacles in life.

Chapter 16: Self-Sabotage - This chapter explores how an internal, contradictory force, fueled by unreleased old commitments, can lead to self-sabotaging behaviors that undermine conscious goals.

Chapter 17: Emotional Blockages - This chapter examines how ancient pacts and vows can create invisible barriers in the emotional realm, leading to persistent negative feelings like sadness, fear, or distrust.

Chapter 18: Life Limitations - This chapter discusses how the subtle influence of spiritual commitments can manifest as concrete limitations in areas such as financial prosperity, physical health, relationships, and life purpose.

Chapter 19: The Shadow of the Past - This chapter synthesizes the persistent, unconscious influence of unresolved commitments as a "shadow of the past" that follows individuals, preventing full presence and peace.

Chapter 20: Signs of the Pact - This chapter guides readers on how to identify concrete signs and clues of active ancient commitments in their own lives through self-analysis, synchronicities, dreams, and intuitive responses.

Chapter 21: Spiritual Memory - This chapter explores accessing deeper spiritual memory, including past life recollections and soul agreements, to understand the origins of persistent challenges and limiting pacts.

Chapter 22: Inherited Bonds - This chapter discusses spiritual bonds inherited from ancestral family lineages, including karmic patterns and unresolved pacts that can affect descendants.

Chapter 23: Retrieving the Past - This chapter provides guidance on actively engaging with past memories of pacts through compassionate inner work, recognizing, honoring, and releasing obsolete commitments.

Chapter 24: Spiritual Autonomy - This chapter emphasizes the inherent power and authority of each soul to modify or end commitments that no longer serve its growth, and warns against external exploitation.

Chapter 25: Free Decision - This chapter focuses on the conscious and sovereign decision to break free from old pacts and vows, affirming one's free will to redirect personal energy and rewrite spiritual contracts.

Chapter 26: Breaking Ties - This chapter provides practical energetic techniques and visualizations for directly cutting or dissolving the subtle bonds that have sustained old, limiting commitments.

Chapter 27: Symbolic Ritual - This chapter explains the value of performing personal symbolic rituals to consolidate the breaking of pacts and anchor the new reality of freedom in tangible reality.

Chapter 28: Forgiveness and Release - This chapter highlights the essential role of deep and sincere forgiveness (of self and others) in releasing lingering emotional residues tied to old pacts for complete liberation.

Chapter 29: Spiritual Protection - This chapter guides readers on how to establish consistent practices of spiritual protection to safeguard newfound freedom and maintain a clear, strong energetic field.

Chapter 30: Self-Transformation - This chapter describes the profound metamorphosis experienced through the process of releasing old pacts, leading to lightness, self-possession, and the blossoming of authentic potential.

Chapter 31: Spiritual Freedom - This chapter defines spiritual freedom as an expansive state of lightness, clarity, and autonomy, where the soul is unencumbered by past ties and guided by conscious choice.

Chapter 32: The Path Ahead - This chapter offers guidance on sustaining newfound freedom, cultivating conscious presence, and wisely making new commitments in alignment with one's evolved truth.

Prologue

There are forces in your life that cannot be explained by logic. Cycles that repeat themselves. Decisions that slip beyond your control. Emotions that arise out of nowhere, bonds that seem rooted in lands you have never set foot on. You have felt all of this. And no, it is not coincidence. There is an invisible architecture governing the course of your existence — and you have built it with your own voice.

Most people go through life without ever realizing that their words, spoken in their most fragile or passionate moments, can become spiritual shackles. In moments of despair, love, fear, or absolute faith, we make commitments. Vows made on one's knees in silent hospitals, promises cast into the wind on nights of anguish, oaths whispered through tears of regret. Words lost in time, yet never erased from the subtle field of the soul.

You may not remember — but your soul does. Because those words carried intention. And intention is energy. And energy... shapes realities.

Throughout your journey, how many pacts have you made? How many vows have you taken without understanding their reach? How many "forevers" have you spoken? And above all, how many do you still carry, invisibly, as chains that limit your present and sabotage your future?

This book is more than just a reading. It is a portal. A deep dive into the hidden realm of the commitments you have sealed — and which, though forgotten, still rule the backstage of your life. It reveals with clarity and depth the workings of a subtle mechanism that most never perceive: that of spiritual vows, emotional pacts, ancestral agreements, and unresolved promises.

Here, each page is a key. Each chapter, a mirror. You are not facing abstract theories, but energetic truths that explain why certain doors remain closed, why some patterns cannot be broken, and why, at times, success, love, or peace seem so close... and yet remain out of reach.

More than an exposition, this is a manual for reclamation. You will learn how to recognize the pacts that still reverberate in your life, even those made in other existences. You will uncover the spiritual roots of emotional blockages, karmic repetitions, and invisible sabotages. With each word, you will feel the real possibility of cutting the threads that bind you to obsolete commitments, restoring your spiritual freedom.

And more: within these pages, you will find not only understanding, but pathways. Rituals, practices, and subtle guidelines that allow you to consciously and truthfully undo what was once sealed with pain, fear, or need. Here, the sacred meets the practical. The invisible becomes clear. What was hidden is revealed.

This book was written for those who sense there is something more. Who intuit that their suffering is not merely the fruit of chance. Who perceive, even without knowing how to explain, that there exists a kind of unwritten contract defining their limits — and that the time has come to renegotiate with the universe.

As you move through these pages, you will not simply read a book. You will be touched by it. Because it awakens, at deep levels, the memories of the soul. It does not matter whether you consider yourself spiritual or skeptical — this content transcends any belief. It speaks to a part of you that knows. That has always known. That was merely waiting to be heard.

It is time to remember. To free yourself. To transform. The words you once spoke in the name of pain, faith, or love no longer need to imprison you. They can be redefined, dissolved, transmuted.

Allow yourself to cross this portal. Awaken to the awareness of the bonds that connect you to the invisible. And discover, with courage and compassion, the immense power you possess — to undo what no longer serves, to restore your sovereignty, and to walk, at last, with lightness.

This book is a compass. A calling. An act of healing.

Read with an open heart.
Life will never be the same again.
Luiz Santos
Editor

Chapter 1
Desperate Cry

There are moments when life corners us, pushing us against cold, impenetrable walls. The ground seems to slip from beneath our feet, the air grows thin, and every familiar door slams shut with a final, resounding thud. It is in this dead end of the soul, where logic dissolves and hope withers, that a different kind of voice rises from the depths of one's being. It is not a casual request, not a random plea cast into the void. It is a primal scream, a roar torn from the very entrails of anguish, directed at any force, any consciousness, any echo in the vast and silent universe that might hear. In that moment of existential fracture, when control slips through trembling fingers and the future looms like a dark abyss, the human spirit, in its utter helplessness, turns to an ancestral resource: the promise born of panic, the pact sealed with tears and the ultimate force of despair.

Picture the scene: the harsh fluorescent light of a hospital corridor, the monotonous beeping of machines marking a funeral rhythm, the antiseptic smell mingling with the subtle fragrance of fear. There, beside a bed where a loved one's life slips away like fine sand, someone falls to their knees—not as a ritual, but because their legs give way. Their gaze drifts aimlessly to the white ceiling, the dusty corners, the emptiness that seems to swallow everything. The words that escape are faltering, hoarse, laden with brutal sincerity. "Let him live," they whisper. "Let her breathe again, and I... I will change everything. I'll abandon my vices, devote every spare hour to helping others, become the person I never managed to be. Just... bring them back." There are no visible witnesses—perhaps only the attentive silence of the night or the intangible presence of something greater—but the intensity of that vow reverberates within the confined space, carried by the raw energy of anguish and wounded love. The promise becomes a sacred contract, signed with the soul in that moment of extreme vulnerability.

Or picture the man sitting at the kitchen table, head in his hands beneath the dim glow of a single lamp. Bills pile up like an avalanche of relentless paper and numbers, the eviction notice lying cold on the worn wood. His family sleeps in the next room, unaware of the approaching storm. He feels the weight of the world on his shoulders—shame, helplessness. Deep within, a desperate negotiation begins. "If I can get out of this," he swears to the dancing shadows, "if a solution appears, I will never repeat the same mistakes. Never again will I yield to gambling, extravagance, or reckless risks. I will live simply, with integrity. I just need one chance, a single lifeline." The promise is made in silence, but with a force that seems to make the very air vibrate. It is an anchor cast into the darkness, hoping to find solid ground, a foothold to prevent the imminent shipwreck. Each word becomes a brick in the construction of a commitment that seems to transcend mere intention.

Even in the whirlwind of sudden danger—a looming accident, the threat of violence, the uncontrolled fury of nature—this cry may arise. In the frozen instant where life and death dance perilously close, the mind races in search of salvation. "If I survive this, if I make it through," the thought echoes like a silent thunder, "I will never complain about life again; I will cherish every second; I will make peace with those I've hurt. Just save me!" It is an instinctive bargain, an attempt to offer something of value—one's future conduct, eternal gratitude—in exchange for continued existence. Adrenaline, panic, and the overwhelming will to live amplify the power of this internal declaration, transforming it into a powerful vow, branded into consciousness at that critical moment.

What makes human beings believe that such promises, made under the crushing weight of circumstance, might have any real effect? Perhaps it is a remnant of magical thinking, an inheritance from ancient times when people believed they could appease angry gods with sacrifices and vows. Perhaps it is the highest expression of faith—the belief that there is a higher order, attentive and responsive to the most sincere cries of the heart. Or perhaps it is simply a reflection of our intrinsic need to find meaning and agency, even when faced with chaos and helplessness. By making a promise, by solemnly committing, the person feels they are doing something, that they are actively participating in the resolution of their dilemma, even if this participation occurs on an invisible plane. The act of vowing becomes a psychological turning point, a statement of hope against all evidence.

Regardless of rational explanation, the experiential truth is that these vows, made in critical moments, carry extraordinary emotional weight. They are not empty words. They are infused with the concentrated energy of fear of loss, the burning desire for salvation, the deep pain of despair. This emotional intensity acts as a catalyst, granting the words a weight and resonance that transcend mere verbal communication. It is as if the very soul is engaged in that declaration, endowing it with a binding force that the conscious mind, in calmer moments, may not fully comprehend. The commitment becomes powerful not only because of the solemnity of the act, but because of the life force invested in it during that existential crisis. The person feels, viscerally, that they have given their word in a definitive way.

And here lies a profound mystery—an idea hinted at by many spiritual and intuitive traditions: such promises, even when born under emotional duress, may indeed create real energetic bonds. It is as if the intensity of the moment, combined with the force of the pledged word, generates a signature in the subtle fabric of reality—a kind of unwritten contract filed away on some level of existence. The urgency may pass, the crisis may be overcome—the child may recover, the debt may be paid, the danger may be avoided—but the echo of that promise remains. The energetic bond created at that moment of outcry does not automatically dissolve with the resolution of the problem. It persists, often forgotten by the conscious mind, yet active in the psyche's background—a silent thread that continues to tie the person to the commitment made in desperation. This subtle bond, though intangible to ordinary senses, may continue to exert a quiet influence, shaping choices, attracting circumstances, or generating inexplicable feelings long after the original storm has subsided.

This invisible thread that lingers is not merely a trick of the imagination or a sentimental illusion: it acts like a seed buried in the deep soil of consciousness, waiting for the right conditions to sprout. Life may resume its course, routines may rebuild, and even the memory of that moment of outcry may dissipate like mist under the sun. Yet something within endures. A subtle unease, an unexpected impulse toward greater honesty, a spontaneous gesture of generosity that seems to arise from nowhere—all these may be expressions of the ancient pact still reverberating, drawing attention to a part of us that made a profound commitment. Sometimes, the promise returns as a whisper in the sleepless night; at other times, as an inexplicable discomfort when faced with a wrong choice. Its presence is discreet but undeniable, like a silent compass that, even relegated to the back of a drawer, continues to point toward something essential.

There are also those who renounce these commitments once the storm has passed, attempting to rationalize their words as the product of a moment of weakness. And yet, the breaking of these promises carries an invisible cost: a kind of internal fracture, a breach of integrity that, even if ignored, exacts a price in the form of discouragement, disorientation, or a vague sense of having lost oneself. Because ultimately, these words spoken at the peak of vulnerability are not addressed solely to the universe or to some transcendent force—they are directed at a deeply intimate and authentic part of the one who utters them. To deny them is to deny that part of oneself. Thus, fulfilling the promise made in the darkness is not merely a matter of loyalty to the "other"—whether divine, symbolic, or imagined—but a way of honoring oneself, of reclaiming the inner cohesion shattered by pain.

In this way, pacts born of desperation, though forged under the pressure of chaos, can become fundamental milestones along the journey of life. They are like small beacons that, even when left behind, continue to emit their faint light, guiding future paths. To fulfill them or not is a choice—but recognizing the weight they carry, the depth of their origin, and the energy that sustains them is, in itself, a step toward a broader understanding of what it means to live in truth. For at the heart of these vows lies a spark of something sacred: the moment when a human being, stripped of all masks, faces the abyss and, instead of surrendering to silence, chooses to speak—and in speaking, is transformed.

Chapter 2
Pacts and Vows

The human word, this seemingly ordinary and everyday tool, holds a latent power that we rarely fully grasp. We use it to describe the world, express feelings, share ideas, yet we often forget its capacity to create, to shape reality, to bind the very speaker to the fabric of their declarations. When intention merges with resolute verbalization, especially in moments of great personal significance or under the weight of overwhelming emotion, the word transcends its communicative role and acquires an almost magical quality—a force capable of sealing destinies and tracing paths along the journey of the soul. It is within this sacred territory of the committed word that we encounter different forms of commitment, nuances of the same primordial force that allows us to make agreements with ourselves, with others, and at times, with the invisible dimensions of existence. Though distinct in form and solemnity, these expressions share a common core: they represent an assumed commitment, a directed energy seeking manifestation.

Perhaps the most familiar of these forms is the promise. It dwells in the realm of daily life, weaving threads of trust and expectation into human interactions.

We promise to arrive on time, to return a borrowed book, to change an unwanted habit. Often, these are informal declarations, expressions of future intention, spoken lightly or with deep sincerity. "I promise I will do my best," we say, and in that instant, we cast a small seed of will into the universe. The strength of a promise resides largely in the integrity of the one who speaks it and in the emotional energy invested. A heartfelt promise, even if simple, carries a vibration of honesty and the desire to fulfill. However, its often more fluid nature can render it susceptible to forgetfulness or reevaluation, though even the lightest promises may leave an energetic trace—a gentle reminder in the field of consciousness of the word once given. It is a commitment that appeals to personal responsibility, a thread we weave between present intention and future action.

Raising the level of solemnity, we encounter the oath. Here, the word takes on greater weight, a formality that distinguishes it from the everyday promise. To swear often involves invoking something sacred or fundamental as witness or guarantor of the commitment. "I swear on my honor," "I swear to God," "I swear upon this symbol." These invocations imbue the act with a dimension that goes beyond interpersonal agreement; it is an alignment of individual will with a higher principle, a truth considered inviolable. Frequently, oaths are made in formal or public contexts—consider oaths of office, the Hippocratic oath taken by physicians, or even passionate declarations where one swears loyalty or vengeance "until the grave." The very structure of the oath suggests a stronger bond, an intention to render the word irrevocable. Breaking it is seen not merely as a character flaw, but as a violation of something deeper, a breach of trust with the very entity invoked as guarantor. The energy of an oath is, by nature, denser, more focused, establishing a stricter program within the consciousness of the one who swears.

Venturing into more intimate and spiritual spheres, we encounter the vow. While the oath often looks outward, seeking validation or witness, the vow frequently turns inward—toward one's relationship with faith, spiritual path, or highest ideals. The monastic vows of poverty, chastity, and obedience are classic examples, representing a voluntary renunciation of certain worldly aspects in favor of total spiritual dedication. Yet vows are not limited to the cloister. A person may vow to serve a humanitarian cause, to follow a particular religious precept with rigor, to devote their life to the pursuit of truth or beauty. Often, the vow involves a devotional exchange: a personal sacrifice, a continuous dedication offered in pursuit of blessings, protection, or spiritual growth. There is a quality of surrender in the vow—a consecration of one's life or a part of it to a purpose that transcends the immediate self. It resonates with particular depth within the soul, as it often touches upon spiritual identity and the ultimate meaning of existence for the one who makes it.

Finally, we arrive at the pact. This term carries the strongest connotation of a bilateral agreement, an explicit negotiation with terms, conditions, and often clear consequences for noncompliance. If the promise is a statement of intention and the oath a solemn affirmation, the pact resembles a firm energetic contract. It implies an exchange, a "I give so that you may give" (do ut des) established in a more concrete form. While promises, oaths, and vows may be made unilaterally (the person committing themselves to an ideal, deity, or personal principle), the pact more strongly suggests the presence of two or more parties involved in the agreement. These parties may be other people, but from a spiritual perspective, may also include non-physical intelligences—entities, forces of nature, archetypal energies. Legends and folklore abound with tales of Faustian pacts—agreements with dark beings in exchange for power or knowledge—but the notion of a pact can also encompass less dramatic arrangements, such as spiritual alliances made with guides or protectors, where mutual responsibilities are established. The essence of the pact lies in the clarity of the agreement and in the binding force it creates between the parties, forming a particularly robust and defined energetic bond.

 Despite these nuances distinguishing promise, oath, vow, and pact, a deeper perspective reveals their fundamental unity. All these forms of commitment are, in essence, energetic contracts. They are born from the powerful conjunction of focused intention and spoken word—whether uttered aloud, whispered in secret, or firmly declared in the silence of the heart. In articulating a commitment, the individual shapes and directs their own vital energy, creating a vibrational pattern, a code inscribed in their personal field, which tends to attract the circumstances necessary for its manifestation or resolution. The spoken word becomes an active force, a command issued to one's own consciousness and, in some mysterious way, to the universe as well. It is human will exercising its creative power through the vehicle of language charged with meaning and emotion.

This understanding of the intrinsic power of the committed word is not new. Throughout history and across various cultures, the given word has always been vested with an aura of moral and mystical power. From sacred oaths sealing alliances between ancient tribes to solemn vows pronounced in religious rituals, to curses and blessings that depended on the force of the invoked word, humanity has intuited and respected the weight of verbal commitments. In many traditions, breaking an oath or vow was considered a grave transgression, capable of attracting not only social condemnation but also spiritual or karmic consequences. This ancestral reverence points to an innate wisdom about the real impact our firm declarations may have—a recognition that words, once released with intention and conviction, weave invisible threads that shape both our inner and outer realities.

It is within this context of ancestral reverence and energetic impact that the true reach of the committed word becomes evident. When one enters a pact or utters a vow, they are not merely performing a symbolic or spiritual act—they are, in fact, activating an invisible mechanism that connects internal and external dimensions of existence. The word becomes an anchor between worlds, between what is and what is yet to be. And this is why so many accounts of personal transformation are intertwined with promises made at moments of rupture, with vows sealed amid suffering or ecstasy. Life often responds—subtly and indirectly—to words spoken in truth. They begin to function as silent compasses, guides that redirect the course of actions, thoughts, and even the synchronicities that unfold in daily life. A verbal commitment, when authentic, reverberates within the very structure of reality, and this resonance persists even when conscious memory no longer recalls its origins.

Thus, it is not a matter of superstition or naive romanticism, but of a profound mechanism of alignment between intention and manifestation. The committed word functions as a fusion point between desire and destiny. Through it, human beings shape their free will, tracing with their own voice the contours of their path. And the clearer, more emotionally charged, and more aligned with inner values that word is, the greater its transformative power. This explains why vows and pacts made in heightened emotional states—intense pain, absolute love, unshakable faith—tend to mold life with almost inevitable force. In those moments, the soul becomes permeable, the ego yields to essence, and the declaration made echoes like a decree in the subtle space. For this reason, every verbal commitment, no matter how intimate, calls for discernment, for it carries within it the potential to become a living seed in the soil of destiny.

Thus, to understand and honor the power of pacts, vows, promises, and oaths is more than respecting a symbolic tradition: it is to recognize the capacity we have to co-create our own experiences through conscious speech. And perhaps this is the deepest invitation contained in this understanding—that we take care with what we say with intention, that we remain faithful to the promises that truly matter, and that we know, with humility and courage, how to revisit or reaffirm our commitments when necessary. For the word that is born from the heart and sustained by action not only transforms the world around us, but reveals, in every fulfillment, who we truly are.

Chapter 3
The Power of the Word

Words float in the air, dissolve into silence, fill pages, yet we rarely pause to feel their true weight, their invisible substance. When spoken with pure intention, with the whole soul behind their utterance, they cease to be mere sonic or graphic symbols. They transform into vehicles of power, bridges between the inner world of thought and will and the vast tapestry of manifested reality. Especially when formalized into firm promises, solemn oaths, or profound vows, words acquire an intrinsic force—a capacity to echo beyond the moment, inscribing their message upon the subtle layers of existence. This is not merely about psychology or social obligation; there is an energetic dynamic at play, a delicate alchemy where human consciousness, through language, interacts with the creative forces of the universe.

When we declare "I promise" or "I swear" with genuine conviction, we are not merely communicating an intention. We are, in a very real sense, releasing a specific creative energy. It is as if the concentration of will, focused at that point of commitment, generates a directed wave of energy—a vibrational emission carrying the essence of that decision. Consider the difference between casually saying "maybe I'll do it" and affirming fervently "I swear I will." The second statement mobilizes much deeper internal resources—emotion, determination, mental focus. This mobilization is not simply an internal psychological event; it radiates outward, imprinting upon the personal energy field and potentially upon the surrounding environment the mark of that resolution. It is an act of co-creation, wherein we use our divine spark to decree a future reality or state of being.

The spiritual perspective offers a key to understanding this phenomenon: words possess vibration. Just as musical notes create distinct harmonies and resonances, words carry unique energetic frequencies. Sounds, when articulated with intention, become more than mere phonemes; they function as codes, keys capable of accessing and influencing different levels of personal and transpersonal reality. When we formalize a commitment through words charged with meaning and emotion, we are essentially programming a specific code into our own energetic system. The words "love," "hatred," "forgiveness," "revenge," "poverty," or "service," when embedded in an oath or vow, are not merely abstract concepts; they become vibrational root notes that resonate within us, attracting or repelling experiences according to their frequency. The universe, in its intrinsic intelligence, seems to respond to these vibrations when they are emitted with strength and clarity.

In this sense, an oath or vow functions as a powerful command. First, it is a command directed at one's own consciousness—both the waking mind and the deeper layers of the subconscious. By solemnly swearing something, we instruct our inner being to align with that directive. The subconscious mind, which largely operates through established programs and beliefs, tends to accept these fervent commands as operative truths. Thus, the oath installs a program that seeks its own fulfillment, influencing automatic thoughts, emotional reactions, and even behaviors in order to carry out the original decree. It is like installing new software into the psyche—a program that runs silently in the background, guiding actions. Simultaneously, this command seems to reverberate beyond the individual, as a signal emitted to the universe—a declaration of intent so potent that the greater field of existence may, in some way, register and mirror this energy, facilitating or obstructing pathways in accordance with the content of the oath.

We see this clearly in poignant examples from human experience. How many people, after a devastating betrayal, have declared through tears and anger: "I will never love anyone again! I will never trust again!"? This phrase, born of extreme pain, is not merely a momentary outburst. It can embed itself deeply within the psyche, becoming an unconscious mantra that governs future interactions. Years later, the person may desire a new relationship, yet encounter an inexplicable internal resistance, a difficulty in opening up, in trusting—as if a part of them is still obeying that ancient decree to close the heart. Likewise, someone who survives a life-threatening situation and swears, "If I get through this, I will dedicate my life to helping others," may feel a constant unease in any other career path, a persistent calling to fulfill that promise made in a moment of distress. The phrase, spoken with fervor and gratitude for spared life, has implanted itself as a near-sacred purpose, a directive the soul seeks to honor. These words become part of the person's energetic identity, silently repeating their command over the years.

It is helpful to visualize each firm promise, each solemn oath, each sincere vow as an energetic seed. At the moment when words are uttered with concentrated intention and emotion, this seed is planted in the fertile soil of consciousness and the personal energy field. Conviction acts as the soil that receives it, emotion as the water that nourishes it. This seed contains the full potential of the assumed commitment—the nature of the promise, its conditions, its expectations. Once planted, it does not remain inert. Like any seed, it holds an intrinsic tendency to grow, to germinate, to seek the light of manifestation. Even if the conscious mind forgets the act of planting, the seed remains alive at the subconscious or energetic level, awaiting the right conditions to sprout or exerting a subtle influence from its invisible roots.

This influence manifests in various ways throughout life. The energetic seed of an oath may attract synchronicities, encounters, or challenges that confront the individual with the theme of their commitment. It may generate feelings of guilt or discomfort when considering actions contrary to the given word, even if circumstances have drastically changed. It may create subtle blocks in areas of life that contradict the old vow—for example, a vow of poverty hindering prosperity, or a lifelong oath of loyalty to someone preventing the formation of new deep emotional bonds. The force of the word pledged in the past continues to operate in the present, not as an inescapable curse, but as an active energy seeking resolution or fulfillment. The future, in this sense, is not a completely virgin territory; it is influenced by the seeds we plant through our most powerful declarations.

Thus, to understand the word as a shaping force of destiny is not a poetic abstraction but a call to conscious responsibility. Each time we verbalize an intention charged with emotion and meaning, we are sowing the field of reality with a specific type of energy that, sooner or later, will demand coherence from us. When we declare something fervently—whether in moments of pain, euphoria, or spiritual clarity—it is as if we leave a footprint imprinted on the invisible ground of existence, a mark that connects us to that version of ourselves who once believed, desired, or desperately needed that spoken truth. To ignore this is to neglect our own active participation in the course life takes, as if we speak to the wind without recognizing that the wind listens—and responds.

This awareness also invites us to revisit the old words that still live within us. Not every vow must be kept, nor every forgotten promise ignored. Sometimes the fairest path is to acknowledge that a vow made under extreme circumstances no longer serves our growth, and then to dissolve it with the same degree of consciousness with which it was made. The power of the word lies, in part, in its constant renewal: we may reconsecrate, reformulate, release. But to do so, we must listen carefully to the voices that still echo within—the phrases we once spoke, which to this day subtly shape our choices and emotions. Making peace with these ancient pacts, honoring or reshaping them, is an act of internal sovereignty—a gesture of spiritual maturity.

Thus, the power of the word lies not only in the eloquence with which it is spoken, but in the coherence with which it is lived. When we speak with clarity, intention, and responsibility, we become conscious co-authors of our existence. And by recognizing the creative power inherent in each committed word, we access a deeper dimension of freedom—the freedom that arises from the alignment between what we say, what we feel, and what we do. For in the end, it is this vibrational integrity that sustains true transformation—not as a sudden event, but as a silent path where each step echoes what we once vowed to become.

Chapter 4
Spiritual Bargaining

At the crossroads of despair, when familiar paths prove fruitless and the shadow of loss or ruin looms large, the human soul instinctively seeks dialogue with the invisible. No longer just a piercing cry for help, but an attempt to establish terms, to propose an exchange, to engage in a negotiation with the forces that seem to govern destiny. It is the ancestral impulse of spiritual bargaining, a phenomenon as old as the very awareness of human finitude and dependency before the mystery of life. Confronted with powerlessness, the individual resorts to a strategy that is almost commercial, applied to the sacred: to offer something of personal value—a life change, an act of devotion, a sacrifice—in exchange for divine intervention, a miracle, or a favorable turn of fortune. It is the mind's attempt to find logic and order even amidst chaos, seeking to establish an agreement where only surrender or silent faith once seemed possible.

The scene is timeless, repeated countless times throughout history and in individual lives. Someone in deep distress—whether facing the grave illness of a child, the imminent threat of financial ruin, or mortal danger—raises their thoughts or voice in a direct proposition to higher realms. "If you heal my child," they fervently promise, "I will build a chapel in your honor," or "I will make an annual pilgrimage to your shrine." The entrepreneur on the brink of collapse may swear: "If I can save my business, I will donate a significant share of the profits to charity and become a fairer employer." The person cornered by violence or natural disaster may cry out: "Save me from this, and I promise to abandon my bad habits, live righteously, and serve a higher purpose." The structure is clear: a condition ("if you grant me this...") followed by an offer ("then I will do that..."). It is an attempt to transform the relationship with the divine or with destiny into a transaction, where help is not merely requested but purchased through a future commitment.

    This impulse to trade, though it may seem naïve or even presumptuous to a purely rational mind, is deeply human and understandable. It arises from the overwhelming sensation of lacking control. When all practical actions fail, when medical science shrugs its shoulders, when economic circumstances seem irreversible, the need to do something becomes pressing. Bargaining offers that sense of agency. By proposing an agreement, the person feels they are actively participating in the solution, contributing their part to influence the outcome. It is a way to channel anguish and hope into concrete action, even if that action is a future commitment made on the plane of intention and word. This need to establish agreements with higher powers is visible in ancestral rituals of offerings to ensure good harvests or protection from enemies, reflecting a fundamental belief in the possibility of interaction and negotiation with the cosmos.

From an energetic and psychological perspective, this bargain is not inconsequential. It creates, in fact, a powerful psychological and spiritual contract. Psychologically, the act of promising something in exchange for help can generate immediate relief from anxiety, providing a focal point of hope and a structure for faith. The person feels they have "done their part," having established a link with a source of power capable of intervening. Spiritually, the emotional intensity and clarity of intention invested in the bargain function as previously discussed: they create an energetic bond, a vibrational signature. The person begins to believe firmly that they have established a commitment not only with themselves but with the subtle forces invoked—be it God, a specific saint, their spiritual guides, or simply the immanent intelligence of the universe. This contract, even if unilaterally proposed, begins to operate in the individual's consciousness as a real and binding agreement.

Narratives illustrating this dynamic are common and resonate deeply within collective experience. How many stories exist of people who, after miraculously escaping death in an accident or overcoming an illness deemed incurable, radically transformed their lives, dedicating themselves to spiritual paths or altruistic causes? Often, behind this transformation lies a fervent vow made on a sickbed or in a moment of panic—a bargain in which life was offered back in exchange for life itself. The individual feels not only grateful but ethically obligated to fulfill their part of the perceived agreement. The promise becomes a new moral compass, guiding future choices and actions as payment of a sacred debt incurred at the moment of greatest need. These stories reinforce belief in the effectiveness of bargaining and in the seriousness of commitments made under such circumstances.

However, this practice of spiritual bargaining invites deeper reflection on its unwritten terms and on the nature of the parties involved. Who, or what, exactly, is on the other side of this negotiation? Is it a personal entity with desires and expectations, who accepts or rejects the offer? Is it the universal law of cause and effect, where the intention to change generates a corresponding response? Or is the bargain primarily a psychological mechanism that focuses the individual's energy, enabling them to access internal resources or perceive solutions previously obscured by despair? And how does the universe, or the divine, respond to these attempts at exchange? Does divine grace operate on the basis of negotiated merits, or does it flow independently of our offers? These are questions that touch the core of various theological and spiritual understandings. The bargain, in attempting to bring mystery into the familiar realm of a commercial agreement, may oversimplify a cosmic dynamic that is far more complex—one based on principles such as unconditional love, learning, and evolution, rather than strictly contractual exchanges. The "unwritten terms" may involve lessons in humility, genuine faith, or acceptance, transcending the logic of the bargain itself.

The way in which the "response" to the bargain manifests is also multifaceted. Sometimes the desired outcome occurs unexpectedly, reinforcing belief in the efficacy of the pact. Other times, the situation resolves by seemingly natural means, leaving it unclear whether the bargain had any influence or whether the individual's shift in attitude and focus opened new pathways. And there are cases where, despite the fervent promise, the expected outcome does not occur, raising questions about the validity of the agreement or the inscrutable designs of destiny. Regardless of the external result, the internal contract remains: the person has made a solemn promise, established an energetic bond with that intention, and this promise will seek expression or resolution within their life.

Thus, spiritual bargaining remains a fascinating expression of the human condition—a blend of vulnerability and audacity, of faith and calculation, of the desire for control and acknowledgment of greater forces. It is the attempt to find common ground with mystery, to use the only true currency we possess—our intention, our word, our future commitment—to negotiate life itself.

This ground, however, is subtle and full of nuance. The risk of spiritual bargaining lies not only in its potential practical ineffectiveness, but in the type of relationship it establishes with the sacred. In viewing the divine as an entity to be persuaded through promises and trades, there is a danger of reducing spirituality to a tool of convenience, activated only in moments of crisis. This does not invalidate the power and legitimacy of vows made in desperation, but invites an expanded awareness: what if true transformation does not reside in the reward or deliverance obtained, but in the very act of committing to something greater? The bargain may be the beginning of a journey, but not its end. What is offered in the heat of the plea may, over time, become not a coin of exchange, but a starting point for a sincere change of course—and perhaps this is its greatest power.

For this reason, the true effectiveness of spiritual bargaining may not lie in convincing the universe to change something outside of us, but in reorganizing ourselves from within. The promise made with a burning soul becomes engraved within as a constant reminder of who we wish to become, and this desire, when honored, has the capacity to reshape the very structure of our experience. Life may not return exactly what was requested, but it often responds to the level of surrender we demonstrate. In fulfilling a promise born of pain, we become more whole, more present, more conscious. And that integrity becomes, in itself, a kind of miracle: a new axis around which existence begins to turn with a different rhythm, a different purpose, a different light.

Thus, spiritual bargaining, more than an attempt at divine bribery, is a mirror revealing the depth of our desire for transformation. It is not about obtaining favors from above, but about rediscovering, in the very act of promising, the forgotten strength of a will aligned with the heart. Even when the response does not come as expected, something moves, something is planted. Because what is truly at stake is not merely the fulfillment of a condition, but the opportunity to make the committed word a point of reconnection between the soul and the mystery that sustains it. And this reconnection, when sincere, holds the power to return us to ourselves.

Chapter 5
Invisible Bonds

Every word pledged with fervor, every promise sealed in the forge of intense emotion, every vow uttered with the soul laid bare, does not simply vanish into the ether once the sound fades. These declarations of commitment, as we have seen, carry creative energy—a vibrational signature inscribed upon the subtle tapestry of existence. But their influence extends beyond a mere momentary echo or mental program. Each of these pacts, vows, and oaths weaves a thread, an invisible bond that energetically connects the individual to the substance of their commitment. It is an ethereal link, imperceptible to the physical senses, yet endowed with surprising tenacity and strength, capable of enduring long past the circumstances that gave birth to it, quietly operating behind the scenes of life.

Imagine these bonds as luminous or shadowy filaments, depending on the nature of the commitment, stretching from the person's essence to the object of their promise. If someone has sworn eternal loyalty to a cause, an energetic thread connects their heart to that force-idea. If they vowed never to trust again after a deep wound, a subtle bond may tie them to that pain and decision, keeping them energetically bound to mistrust.

If they took a vow of poverty in exchange for divine grace, a link may persist, connecting their energy to the vibration of lack. These bonds are not poetic metaphors; from a spiritual perspective, they are considered real energetic structures, existing within the subtle field that interpenetrates and sustains physical reality. Their invisibility to the physical eye does not diminish their functionality or influence in any way.

One of the most intriguing characteristics of these bonds is their ability to persist regardless of conscious memory. A vow made in childhood, during a moment of fear or intense fantasy, may be entirely forgotten by the adult mind. A passionate promise exchanged in youth may have been lost in the mists of time and subsequent experiences. Yet, the energetic bond created in that moment may remain active and vibrant, exerting influence from the deepest layers of being. It operates like a contract filed away in a forgotten drawer of the subconscious or, from a broader perspective, recorded in what some traditions call the Akashic Record—a kind of cosmic library or soul memory where all actions, thoughts, and intentions are stored. There, the record of the pact remains, and the energetic link associated with it continues to connect the soul to that ancient decree, regardless of the time or lifetimes that have passed.

This backstage persistence is what makes these bonds so significant—and at times, so problematic. A vow made decades ago—or even, as we will explore later, in past existences—may actively shape thoughts, emotions, and behaviors in the present life, without the person having the slightest awareness of its origin.

Someone may feel an inexplicable aversion to certain situations, a chronic difficulty in a particular area of life, or a painful relational pattern that keeps repeating, and the root may lie in an invisible bond tied to a forgotten commitment. The subtle link keeps the person energetically connected to the object or condition promised, creating a constant resonance that attracts or sustains circumstances aligned with the original vow. It is like having an internal compass that, unbeknownst to the person, continues to point toward a direction defined long ago.

The comparison to an invisible chain is quite apt. Imagine someone who, in a previous life or during youthful idealism, swore eternal loyalty to a certain political or philosophical ideal. Years later, their experiences and reflections may lead them to question that ideal, to wish to explore new avenues of thought or action. Yet, they may feel enormous internal resistance, great difficulty in breaking away from old beliefs, a sense of guilt or betrayal when contemplating change. It is as if something holds them, an invisible force pulling them back toward their former loyalty. This force may be the energetic bond created by the original oath—the invisible chain still anchoring them to that ideological mast. Likewise, a vow of chastity taken in another era, or even a promise never to give oneself to love again after a trauma, may act as a chain preventing the person from experiencing healthy intimate relationships in the present, even if they consciously desire otherwise.

It is crucial to understand that, despite their intangible nature, these bonds possess real power. They are not mere psychological constructs or fantasies. The energy invested at the moment of commitment, crystallized in the form of a subtle bond, continues to operate and influence the individual's energetic dynamics. This force may manifest as blocks, limitations, repetitive patterns, or even as a diffuse sensation of heaviness or not belonging. Ignoring the possibility of these bonds is like trying to navigate a boat without considering the underwater currents—we may row with all our strength toward the desired direction, yet be continually diverted by unseen forces we do not comprehend.

For this reason, recognizing the potential existence of these invisible bonds is a fundamental step on the journey of self-knowledge and spiritual liberation. As long as we fail to acknowledge that we may be energetically tied to past commitments, we will continue to attribute our difficulties solely to external factors, to bad luck, or to character flaws. By opening the mind to the possibility that subtle ties—woven by our own words and intentions at some point in time—may be influencing our present reality, we gain a new perspective. We begin to see our challenges not as immutable sentences but as possible effects of causes that can be identified and, more importantly, transformed.

This transformation, however, does not occur through mere denial or deliberate forgetting of ancient pacts. It requires a conscious process of review and, often, of release from these invisible bonds. Just as a legal contract demands attention to be dissolved, energetic ties require presence, intention, and, above all, truth. When we honestly revisit the promises we have made—even those we believed long buried—we begin to reclaim the power they still exert over us. In some cases, it is enough to recognize and reaffirm the commitment with renewed awareness. In others, an internal or ritualistic act of revocation is needed—a kind of reconciliation between the part that once made the promise and the part that now wishes to move in a new direction. The symbolic act, when charged with emotional truth, holds the power to break or reconfigure the original energetic thread.

This work of unbinding is not a violent rupture but an act of integration. Rather than severing ties with disdain or rejection, the most effective path is one that embraces the original intention with compassion, understanding the emotional and spiritual context in which the commitment was made. The goal is not to deny who we once were but to free who we have now become. A vow made out of love, fear, or devotion need not be scorned—it may be honored as a necessary step along the journey and then consciously transmuted. The energy once trapped in the bond can thus be redirected toward new creations, new commitments, more aligned with present values and desires. In doing so, we recover fragments of our vital energy that were scattered or imprisoned, strengthening our spiritual autonomy.

To free oneself from an invisible bond is not to forget who one was, but to allow one's own story to be rewritten with freedom and clarity. It is to recognize that what once served as a beacon may now act as an anchor—and that both functions, though opposite, deserve equal respect. In the end, invisible bonds reveal themselves as bridges between past and present—bridges that, when crossed with awareness, lead us back to wholeness. And it is in this reunion with our center that we finally become able to make new vows—freer, clearer, and more aligned with the truth that now pulses alive within us.

Chapter 6
Past Lives

The invisible bonds we weave with our words and intentions, as we have seen, possess a tenacity that defies time and conscious memory. But how far does this persistence extend? If a vow made in childhood can echo into adulthood, is it possible that even older commitments, forged in contexts and eras unknown to our current mind, might still exert their influence over us? To explore this intriguing possibility, we are invited to broaden our perspective on the very nature of identity and the human journey, contemplating the notion that our present existence may be but a chapter in the soul's long saga—a journey through multiple lifetimes. The idea of reincarnation, present in so many cultures and spiritual traditions around the world, offers a fascinating framework for understanding the origin of certain influences and patterns that seem to defy logical explanation within the confines of a single biography.

In this expanded view, spiritual consciousness—the soul, the higher self, the immortal essence—is the perennial traveler moving through different bodies and experiences over the centuries. With each new incarnation, it carries an accumulated baggage: the lessons learned, the personality traits developed, the karmic debts to be resolved, and, crucially for our inquiry, the energetic remnants of solemn commitments undertaken in previous lives. Ancient oaths, vows made under dramatic circumstances, pacts sealed in remote times—all may remain etched in the soul's deep memory, continuing to vibrate and influence the journey long after the original stage has vanished. The current personality may hold no conscious recollection of these past lives, but the soul remembers, and its subtle energetic baggage mysteriously shapes present experience.

Let us imagine the countless possibilities contained within the vastness of human history. Picture a reclusive monk in a medieval monastery, dedicating his existence to God through strict vows of poverty, obedience, and silence. The sincerity and discipline with which he lived these vows may have created a strong energetic imprint on his soul—a signature of renunciation and austerity. Or envision a tribal warrior in an era of constant conflict, swearing eternal vengeance against the clan that wiped out his family, a blood-sealed vow of hatred. The intensity of this promise of retaliation may have forged a powerful energetic bond with the vibration of hostility and loss. Consider also two lovers in times of war or social prohibitions, making a solemn promise of eternal love, vowing that their souls would reunite and remain together forever, even in the face of tragic separation imposed by fate. This passionate vow may have woven an unbreakable bond between their spiritual essences. These are but glimpses of human dramas where oaths and vows may have been uttered with a force capable of echoing through the ages.

These past commitments, as suggested, are recorded in the soul's intrinsic memory, often referred to as the Akashic Records or the Book of Life. They are not mere passive recollections; they are active energetic matrices reverberating across time. The energy invested in the original vow continues to seek expression or resolution. Thus, the soul may be drawn, life after life, to circumstances that mirror or challenge that ancient commitment until the lesson is learned or the bond is consciously dissolved. The monk's vow of poverty may manifest today as an inexplicable struggle with money, an unconscious self-sabotage whenever prosperity seems within reach, even as the person works hard to achieve financial success. The warrior's vow of vengeance may translate into a tendency to attract conflict, harbor deep resentments, or experience disproportionate outbursts of anger without any apparent cause in the present life. The lovers' promise of eternal love may result today in a persistent feeling of something missing, a difficulty in surrendering to new relationships, or a recurring attraction to partners who, in some way, mirror the dynamics of that ancient and perhaps impossible love.

The beauty and complexity of this perspective lie in its ability to give meaning to challenges that might otherwise seem random or unfair. Why does someone so kind and hardworking face such financial difficulties? Why does a person so eager for love seem destined for loneliness or painful relationships? Why do certain fears or blocks persist despite years of conventional therapy? The possibility that we may be under the influence of bonds carried over from other lives opens a new dimension of understanding. It is not a matter of finding excuses or adopting a fatalistic stance, but rather recognizing that our story is far more vast and profound than we imagine, and that the roots of our present challenges may be anchored in very ancient grounds.

Understanding the possibility that pacts and vows can transcend incarnations greatly expands our view of ourselves and the mechanisms of the spiritual journey. We realize that we are not merely the product of our genetics and upbringing in this life, but also the result of a long pilgrimage of the soul, with its choices, lessons, and accumulated commitments. This expanded awareness is profoundly liberating, for it allows us to investigate the deepest layers of our being in search of the origins of our limiting patterns. It prepares us for the work of identifying and ultimately releasing these ancestral bonds, not as a burdensome task, but as a loving act of reclaiming our complete history.

This journey of loving reclamation does not require us to relive the suffering of each past story, but to become aware of the silent forces shaping our choices and emotions. By recognizing these invisible bonds, we take the first step toward transforming them. Healing lies not merely in remembering who we were, but in the wisdom of choosing who we are now. The encounter with old vows need not be a condemnation—it can be an opportunity to rewrite the narrative. When we view our challenges with this compassionate and encompassing gaze, we are able to untie the knots of destiny with gentleness and clear intention.

Each recognition is like a key that opens the doors of the unconscious, allowing imprisoned fragments of our being to return to the natural flow of life. The language of the soul, unlike linear logic, expresses itself through subtle sensations, synchronicities, and intuitions which, if embraced, guide us along a path of reintegration. As we access these internal records, we begin to perceive that our current reality is not merely a reflection of what we experience here and now, but the convergence point of many timelines, all interwoven by the pursuit of learning, balance, and love. From this perspective, even the briefest encounters may carry ancestral weight, and every choice may become a turning point toward freedom.

In doing so, we assume a new role within our own existence: we cease to be victims of circumstances and become conscious healers of our own journey. The awareness of ancient vows is not a prison, but an invitation to true freedom—one born of deep self-knowledge and a commitment to the evolution of the spirit. By bringing these hidden roots to light, we create space for new beginnings—lighter, more conscious—where the ties of the past no longer bind us, but serve instead as a springboard toward a fuller, more authentic life aligned with the soul's purpose.

Chapter 7
The Law of Karma

The soul's journey, with its commitments undertaken and its bonds woven through time, does not unfold in a vacuum of randomness. Just as the physical universe obeys precise laws governing the movement of celestial bodies and the interaction of matter, so too does the moral and spiritual universe seem to operate under ordering principles—subtle laws that ensure a dynamic balance and an evolutionary purpose to all experiences. Among these universal laws, perhaps the most fundamental and widely recognized—though often misunderstood—is the law of karma, the inexorable principle of cause and effect. Understanding this law is essential for grasping the true depth and enduring consequences of the pacts, vows, and oaths we make, as each of these acts of commitment fits perfectly into this vast cosmic mechanism of action and reaction.

At its core, the karmic law posits that every intentional action generates a corresponding consequence. It is not a system of rewards and punishments administered by an external judging entity, but rather a natural law of energetic balance, as impersonal and reliable as the law of gravity. Every thought we cultivate, every word we utter, every action we take with defined intent—all of these are causes that will inevitably produce effects of a similar nature. The energy we emit into the universe, in whatever form, returns to us, shaping our future experiences and weaving the complex tapestry of our personal destiny. It is a mechanism of continuous learning, where we reap precisely what we sow.

In this context, the making of a pact, oath, or vow assumes significant karmic importance. As we have explored, these acts are charged with concentrated intention and emotional force, making them particularly potent causes launched into the field of existence. When someone makes a solemn vow, they are creating a specific cause, emitting a clear vibrational frequency that propagates through the universe. The energy of that promise, of that commitment, immediately begins to seek its manifestation and fulfillment. The act of establishing the commitment is the initial cause.

The consequences, the karmic effects, unfold depending on how we handle the cause we have created. If the commitment is honored and the promise fulfilled with integrity, the energetic cycle tends to complete harmoniously. The emitted energy finds its resolution, and the effect may be consolidated learning, strengthened character, or what we perceive as "blessings" or favorable circumstances aligned with the positive nature of the fulfilled vow. However, if the pact is broken, if the oath is violated, or if the vow is neglected or abandoned without conscious resolution, the energetic situation becomes more complex. The initial cause remains, but the energy emitted becomes blocked, unable to complete its natural circuit.

Here arises the notion of a spiritual debt. According to the karmic law, an unfulfilled vow or broken pact can generate an energetic imbalance that needs to be restored. The energy of the promise, still seeking fulfillment, remains active in the soul's field as an outstanding matter—a kind of energetic debt. It is not a financial debt or divine punishment in the human sense, but rather dissonant energy calling for harmonization, an unfinished task that the soul recognizes at its deepest level. This "debt" represents the energy and intention that were set in motion but have not found their proper resolution.

Until this spiritual debt is settled—whether through the eventual fulfillment of the promise (even symbolically or adapted to new circumstances), through a profound understanding of the lesson involved, or through a conscious act of release and forgiveness that neutralizes the pending energy—the person may repeatedly attract situations confronting them with the central theme of that ancient vow. The karmic law, in its intrinsic wisdom, tends to present us with mirrors of our unresolved causes. Thus, someone who has broken a vow of loyalty may repeatedly encounter situations of betrayal (whether as victim or perpetrator) until they understand the depth of trust and integrity. Someone who has failed to fulfill a promise of serving the needy may experience an inner emptiness or face circumstances that force them to confront their selfishness, until the lesson of compassion and service is fully assimilated. These situations are not punishments, but rather carefully orchestrated opportunities created by the soul itself in concert with karmic law to revisit the issue, comprehend the consequences of a given word, and finally restore balance.

This brings us to the most crucial and liberating aspect of understanding karma: its fundamentally educational nature. Far from being a punitive or vengeful force, karma is a patient and perfect teacher. Its ultimate aim is not suffering, but learning, the evolution of consciousness, and the awakening to responsibility for our own actions, thoughts, and words. If a pact was broken out of ignorance, fear, or weakness, the soul may choose, in its evolutionary journey, to experience challenging circumstances related to that theme—not to be punished, but to develop the qualities that were lacking: willpower, clarity, compassion, integrity. Each challenge encountered becomes a practical lesson about the implications of our commitments and the sacred importance of the spoken word. The pain that may arise in this process is not an end in itself, but rather a catalyst for transformation and growth.

Thus, pacts, vows, and oaths, with all their complex energetic and psychological ramifications, are part of a much larger context of universal harmony. Every commitment we make is a note we add to the cosmic symphony. The law of karma acts as the invisible conductor ensuring that each note eventually finds its place within the overall harmony. It ensures that every cause produces its corresponding effect, that every imbalance is ultimately corrected, and that every lesson is presented until it is fully learned.

Recognizing this profound harmony underlying the operation of karmic law is simultaneously an invitation to humility and responsibility. We are not passive pieces in an arbitrary cosmic game, but attentive co-creators of every step in our evolutionary journey. Every choice, no matter how subtle it may seem, reverberates across layers that extend beyond this present existence, revealing the latent power we hold in speaking, acting, and deciding. Thus, becoming aware of the karmic dimension of the commitments we make is an awakening to a more refined spiritual ethic, where the integrity of intention is as valuable as the act itself, and where every word pledged becomes a seed of future experiences.

This awareness awakens a new way of approaching life's challenges. Instead of lamenting obstacles or resisting pain, we begin to see them as revelations of internal contents calling for recognition and healing. Often, repetitive cycles of suffering or frustration are merely the echoes of misunderstood or unresolved promises, reverberating until they are reintegrated with wisdom. Understanding this allows us to act with greater compassion toward ourselves and others, knowing that each being carries within their soul untold stories, silent pacts that unconsciously shape behaviors and emotions. In this way, the law of karma not only reveals but also guides, offering a secure path toward liberation and realignment with our truest essence.

When we accept responsibility for what we have created—whether consciously or unconsciously—we take a decisive step toward freedom. The karmic law, far from imprisoning, points the way toward the self-regulation of the spirit, where every imbalance may be restored through love, truth, and sincere repentance. With this understanding, every unfulfilled vow ceases to be a curse and becomes an opportunity for reconnection with one's own light. After all, the true purpose of karma is not to punish, but to teach the art of living with awareness, reverence, and coherence, like one who learns, note by note, to play the melody of life with soul.

Chapter 8
Broken Word

The spoken word, like a seal impressed upon the soft wax of the soul, carries with it the weight of intention and the strength of commitment. We have seen how it can create bonds, direct energies, and even echo through lifetimes, becoming part of the great law of cause and effect that governs the spiritual journey. But what happens when this sacred word is broken? What occurs on the subtle level when a pact is not fulfilled, an oath is violated, or a fervent promise is left forgotten? Human frailty, unforeseen life circumstances, a change of heart, or simply the passage of time may all lead to the non-fulfillment of commitments once made with great solemnity. Regardless of the reasons—ranging from the inevitable to the negligent—the breaking of one's word reverberates deeply within the being, generating energetic and karmic consequences that deserve to be understood not with fear, but with clarity and responsibility.

When someone breaks a commitment considered sacred—whether made to oneself, to another person, to a deity, or to an ideal—a process of internal energetic misalignment is set in motion. Think of it as vibrational dissonance. The initial energy, charged with intention and emotion at the moment of the oath, created a specific pattern, a kind of energetic blueprint for the future. When current actions or willpower deviate radically from that original pattern without conscious resolution, a conflict arises. The energy of "I swear I will" collides with the energy of "I did not" or "I will no longer." This internal friction, this misalignment between the established intention and lived reality, is not merely an abstract matter; it can manifest palpably in the individual's experience.

This internal dissonance often translates into unsettling emotional states, even when its origin is not consciously recognized. Diffuse feelings of guilt, a nagging sense of having failed at something important, a seemingly baseless remorse, or even a subtle fear of punishment or negative consequences may emerge. The soul, at its deepest level, recognizes the incongruence—the lack of integrity between the given word and the subsequent action (or inaction). Even if the rational mind rationalizes or forgets the original commitment, the subtle consciousness registers the broken agreement, and this perception may surface as anxiety, heaviness of heart, or persistent self-criticism. One may feel unworthy of happiness or success, as though unconsciously self-punishing for having "broken one's word."

Beyond this internal misalignment, spiritualist perspectives suggest that the failure to fulfill a pact or vow leaves a kind of "loose end" in the individual's energetic field. The invisible bond created by the commitment has been neither honored nor properly dissolved; it remains like an exposed wire, unresolved energy seeking closure. This loose end may function as a point of vulnerability or as an energetic attractor. Like an open circuit seeking to complete itself, this unresolved energy may subtly draw into one's life experiences, relationships, or challenges that mirror the central theme of the broken promise. It is as if life, operating under the aegis of the karmic law of learning, continually offers new opportunities to revisit the issue, to confront the energy of that unfulfilled commitment, and ultimately to find resolution or integration. The repetition of certain painful or limiting patterns may, in some cases, be a sign of these loose ends—unfinished matters at the level of the soul.

This dynamic is closely linked to the notion of karmic debt. As we have seen, the law of cause and effect seeks balance. Breaking a significant oath is a cause that generates an effect of imbalance. This imbalance can be understood as an unresolved lesson, an area where the soul still needs to develop greater understanding, integrity, or responsibility. The "debt" is not owed to an external entity but to oneself—to one's own evolutionary journey. The soul carries this unlearned lesson forward, and karmic law will provide the necessary circumstances—in this life or in future ones—for the lesson to eventually be assimilated. Breaking one's word may thus inscribe in the soul's curriculum the need to learn about the consequences of a lack of integrity, the value of trust, or the power contained in one's own declarations. The difficulties faced later may be seen as "practical lessons" designed to teach this pending lesson.

It is essential to emphasize that exploring these consequences is not intended to frighten or burden anyone with additional guilt. On the contrary, the intention is to illuminate the profound seriousness with which many spiritual traditions regard the spoken word and the importance of personal integrity in the soul's journey. Understanding that our commitments carry energetic weight and karmic consequences invites greater awareness and responsibility when making them. More importantly, it reveals that the difficulties we may face as a result of broken promises are not dead ends but invitations for growth, repair, and the restoration of inner balance. Recognizing the possible link between a present challenge and an unfulfilled past commitment is the first step toward actively seeking harmonization, whether through forgiveness, understanding, reparative acts, or the conscious and loving release of that old bond.

This process of harmonization does not necessarily require the promise to be fulfilled exactly as it was made, especially when life circumstances have made such fulfillment unviable or even counterproductive. What is asked of the soul is authenticity in reviewing its commitments and sincerity in the intention to restore internal integrity. Often, a new conscious choice—aligned with the greater good and with values matured along the way—can serve as a healing response to the broken promise. The symbolic act of acknowledging the break, reflecting on its causes, and lovingly releasing that retained energy is, in itself, a profound gesture of spiritual responsibility, capable of resealing the energetic field with coherence and lightness.

Some traditions suggest specific practices for dealing with these broken bonds, such as forgiveness rituals, release meditations, unsent letters, or even simple moments of introspection in which one declares, with full presence of heart, the intention to consciously and peacefully dissolve the pact. These gestures, however subtle they may seem, possess the power to redirect the energetic flow that had been interrupted. They restore not only balance within the soul's field but also return to the person a sense of dignity and internal coherence, as if the weight of the broken promise were no longer an unconscious burden but instead a marker of learning and renewal. Rather than carrying the stigma of error, the soul begins to resonate with the frequency of transformative responsibility.

Thus, the breaking of one's word need not mark the beginning of a cycle of pain but can represent the threshold of a new phase: more lucid, more compassionate, and deeply reconciled with inner truth. When sincere intention aligns with the understanding of the impact of one's actions, what was once a fracture becomes a turning point. And it is in this humble and powerful gesture of acknowledging and integrating our failures that the soul's journey is strengthened, opening space for new commitments—now more mature, conscious, and aligned with the light that silently always calls us back home.

Chapter 9
Subtle Consequences

The breaking of a pledged word, as we have seen, generates shockwaves that extend beyond the act itself, creating internal misalignments and sowing karmic lessons along the soul's journey. However, the repercussions are not limited to moral and emotional spheres, nor to recurring patterns of life events. There are even more elusive, deeper consequences that operate silently behind the scenes of our energetic and spiritual makeup. These subtle and invisible effects, precisely because of their hidden nature, can be particularly persistent and challenging, undermining our well-being and our ability to fully express ourselves without us even suspecting that their origin lies in an unresolved past commitment. Delving into these deeper layers is essential for a complete understanding of the impact that pacts and vows have on our existence.

One of the most significant consequences on the energetic plane is the creation of blockages. Imagine vital energy—prana, chi—this subtle force that animates our body and consciousness—flowing harmoniously through invisible channels, nourishing every aspect of our being. A broken commitment, especially one charged with strong intention or emotion, can act like a dam within this vital flow. Part of the energy originally invested in the promise becomes "trapped" or stagnant, unable to continue its natural course because the circuit of the commitment was neither completed nor properly dissolved. A point of congestion forms—an energetic knot that impedes the free circulation of life force in that specific area of our system.

These subtle energetic blockages, though undetectable by conventional means, may have diffuse and far-reaching effects across various aspects of life. Someone may feel their spiritual growth stalled, struggling to meditate deeply or to access their intuition, as though an opaque veil separates them from higher dimensions—perhaps the energy needed for such connection is stagnant in an unresolved vow of renunciation. Another person may find their dearest projects mysteriously paralyzed, encountering inexplicable obstacles just when everything seemed to be going well—perhaps the energy of manifestation is blocked by an unconscious pact of self-sacrifice. Even mental clarity may be affected; a persistent fog, difficulty concentrating, or chronic indecision may be symptoms of mental energy trapped in a past oath that generates internal conflict. There may be no apparent cause, but the energetic root lies in the stagnation created by the broken commitment.

Venturing into an even subtler realm, some spiritual traditions speak of the creation of thought-forms. The concentrated and directed mental and emotional force present in a fervent pact may, according to these views, give rise to a type of energetic entity—an elemental thought-form animated by the original intention. This thought-form, born from the individual's own psyche but sustained by the intensity of the vow, might remain active in the person's energy field even after the pact has been forgotten. Its nature would be to mirror and uphold the vibration of the original commitment. Thus, a thought-form created by an oath such as "never to be happy again" could act as a constant energetic reminder of that decision, subtly sabotaging moments of joy or attracting circumstances that validate the original belief. It could even exert a near-autonomous influence, interfering with one's choices whenever they threaten to violate the ancient decree—not out of malice, but from fidelity to its original programming. In cases of collective vows made by groups or families, one may speak of egregores—fields of collective energy that bind members together and perpetuate the energy of the shared commitment.

Beyond personal effects, the energy of these commitments may also impregnate environments or influence relationships. A place where a dramatic oath was made—such as an ancient battlefield, a secluded chapel, or even a room where a deep crisis unfolded—may retain the energetic "memory" of that event. Returning to such a place, even years later, a person may feel an inexplicable chill, a sudden sadness, or relive emotions linked to the original pact, without consciously understanding why. Similarly, individuals who were involved in the original pact, or even their descendants, may carry within their own energy fields an echo of that commitment. Interacting with these people may reactivate the dormant energy of the pact, triggering emotional reactions or behavior patterns that seem to arise "out of nowhere" but are, in truth, resonances of that ancient shared bond.

The crucial point to retain from all these explorations of subtle consequences is this: although invisible to our eyes and often imperceptible to our conscious mind, the energetic and spiritual repercussions of pacts and vows—especially unresolved ones—are real. They operate beneath the surface of daily life, influencing our flow of vital energy, our thoughts, our emotions, and even the environments and relationships that surround us. Attributing persistent difficulties solely to psychological or circumstantial causes may be insufficient if we do not consider these hidden energetic dynamics. Becoming aware of these possibilities—energetic blockages, thought-forms, environmental imprints—is not an exercise in esoteric fantasy but an important step toward a more holistic understanding of ourselves and the challenges we face.

This broader understanding should not serve as an additional burden, but rather as a key to access deeper layers of self-healing and spiritual empowerment. In recognizing that subtle forces influence our experiences, we also gain the opportunity to consciously engage with these forces. We can choose to seek practices that act directly on the energetic field, such as vibrational cleansing, specific release meditations, guided visualizations, and symbolic rituals for closing cycles. The simple act of acknowledging an ancient vow still active, bringing it into the light of consciousness with honesty and an intention to release, may trigger a spontaneous process of dissolution. After all, that which is clearly seen tends to lose the power it held while operating from the shadows.

Often, these subtle blockages do not need to be "eliminated" with force or willpower, but rather understood and embraced with compassion. They are fragments of ourselves, aspects of our being that, at some point, believed they were doing their best by taking on a given commitment. Instead of battling these parts, we can extend them a loving hand, listen to them with respect, and thank them for their loyalty. This gesture of inner reconciliation transforms the energetic field: what was once a knot becomes a bridge; what was once a limitation becomes a lesson. In this more sensitive and spiritualized approach, healing comes not from denial or repression but from the conscious reintegration of all that was once separated by pain, fear, or ignorance.

Thus, understanding the subtle consequences of broken commitments is not an invitation to fear, but a call to presence. A call to be more attentive to the intentions we place in our words, more conscious of the energies we seal with our vows, and more willing to assume, with maturity and serenity, the sacred work of undoing what binds us and restoring the natural flow of life within. It is at this point that spirituality aligns with freedom: when we cease to be victims of hidden forces and become co-creators of our own healing, reclaiming the wholeness of being with courage, awareness, and love.

Chapter 10
Guilt and Fear

The consequences of unresolved pacts and vows, as we have seen, extend their tendrils beyond the visible, creating energetic blockages and subtle reverberations within our personal field. However, perhaps the most immediate and tangible manifestations of these worn or broken bonds reside in the fertile ground of human emotions. Anchored deep within the heart and mind, feelings of guilt and fear often emerge as dark guardians of these ancient commitments, acting as weights that keep us tethered to the past and hinder our progress toward freedom. These emotions, though painful and often paralyzing, are not mere psychological byproducts; from a spiritual perspective, they themselves carry a dense energy and may play a crucial role in keeping active the very ties we seek to break.

Guilt, in particular, functions as a powerful energetic adhesive. When we feel that we have failed to honor a given word—especially one invested with sacredness or spoken in a moment of great intensity—a heavy burden may settle upon our consciousness. We feel that we have disappointed someone or something greater—perhaps the deity invoked in the oath, perhaps a spiritual entity with whom we believe we made an agreement, perhaps another person involved in the promise, or, quite often, ourselves, our own integrity, our ideal of conduct. This sense of failure, of having transgressed a personal or spiritual code, generates a dense energy that paradoxically binds us even more to the memory and vibration of that broken pact. It is as if guilt keeps us chained to the scene of the "crime," internally reliving the sensation of error and inadequacy.

This guilt may manifest in insidious ways. One is unconscious self-punishment. The person who feels guilty for breaking a vow may begin to see themselves as unworthy of happiness, love, or prosperity. They may, without realizing it, sabotage opportunities for joy or success because a part of them believes they do not deserve good things after having "broken their word." Each time happiness knocks at the door, the inner voice of guilt whispers that there is an outstanding debt, an uncorrected wrong, and the person retreats, maintaining a state of suffering or limitation that serves as self-imposed penance. Another manifestation is a constant heaviness of heart—a lingering melancholy, a sense of carrying an invisible burden, even if the specific origin—the broken pact—has been relegated to unconscious oblivion. The energy of guilt continues to vibrate, coloring life's perceptions with gray tones of remorse and inadequacy.

Alongside guilt, or often intertwined with it, arises fear. The fear of the consequences of having violated a sacred commitment is a deeply rooted emotion in many cultures and individual psyches. There is fear of retaliation, of divine or karmic punishment.

Ancestral stories and legends often depict wrathful gods or cruel fates befalling those who dare to break solemn oaths. This cultural heritage, combined with one's own inner sense of having transgressed something important, can generate a diffuse yet persistent fear that something bad will happen. One may fear attracting misfortune, illness, financial loss, or other adversities as direct consequences of their "failure." Even if the rational mind doubts this, a more primitive or superstitious part may remain on alert, anticipating inevitable spiritual reprisal. If the pact involved specific entities, the fear may become even more concrete, focused on the possibility of persecution or negative influence from these beings (a topic to be further explored).

Curiously, fear may also take on a paradoxical form: fear of liberation itself. As uncomfortable or limiting as an old pact may be, it represents familiar territory, a known structure within which the person has learned to live. The prospect of breaking this bond, of facing life without this old (albeit negative) reference point, may evoke a deep fear of the unknown. What will happen if I free myself from this vow? Who will I be without this burden or this identity defined by the pact? The chain, though heavy, may offer a strange sense of safety, and the idea of releasing it may feel frightening. The fear of claiming one's autonomy, of assuming full responsibility for the present without the "excuse" of the past, may be as great an obstacle as the fear of punishment.

It is essential to recognize these feelings of guilt and fear as understandable emotional locks, but ultimately, as surmountable ones. They are natural human reactions to the perception of having failed at an important commitment or to the fear of the unknown. However, as long as we allow these emotions to dominate us, they will continue to bind us to the past, reinforcing the energetic ties we wish to dissolve. Guilt keeps us focused on the mistake, preventing forgiveness and self-acceptance. Fear paralyzes us, preventing courageous action toward freedom.

Exposing this emotional dimension is crucial because the release from pacts and vows is not merely a technical act of cutting energetic cords or performing rituals. It is an integral process that also demands healing of the heart. It requires that we confront our guilt, understand it within its original context, and offer ourselves compassion and forgiveness. It requires that we face our fears, question their origins, and learn to transmute them into trust—trust in our ability to handle the unknown, trust in the benevolence of the universe, trust in our innate right to freedom and happiness.

These emotions, when approached with maturity and loving awareness, can cease to be anchors and become gateways. Guilt, for instance, when understood not as condemnation but as a signal that deep values were neglected, can reconnect us to our essential integrity. From there, no longer as executioner but as moral compass, it points the way toward inner reconciliation. Fear, in turn, when faced honestly, often reveals itself as a mask of the unknown—a fertile space of potential where true transformation may occur. It is not a matter of denying these emotions or rushing their dissolution, but of creating an inner space where they can be seen, felt, and ultimately transcended.

It is within this delicate territory that the deepest spiritual work takes place: not in the absence of difficult emotions, but in the willingness to transform them into foundations for a new stage of the journey. Each time we dare to forgive ourselves, even without external guarantees of absolution, we give the soul a chance to regenerate. Each time we choose to trust, despite the internal trembling, we open the doors to experiences more aligned with our present state of consciousness, no longer governed by echoes of the past. In doing so, we become less prisoners of old pacts and more conscious authors of our own path. And it is in this exercise of loving responsibility that true liberation begins—a freedom that does not demand forgetting the past but integrating it with wisdom.

Thus, freeing oneself from the guilt and fear linked to old commitments is not about erasing the story, but illuminating it. It is about reclaiming the dignity we may have felt we lost and discovering that, even within broken vows, there once lived a sincere desire to do right, to grow, to love. In recognizing this, we may embrace the version of ourselves that erred with the same tenderness we would offer a frightened child. And it is within this gesture of self-embrace that the chains loosen—not by force, but because they no longer make sense in the light of the new truth we have chosen to live.

Chapter 11
Spiritual Entities

Our journey toward understanding pacts, vows, and oaths has led us to explore the power of the word, the invisible bonds it weaves, its karmic reverberations, and the emotions it stirs. Until now, we have primarily focused on commitment as an act of the soul itself, an energetic contract with oneself or with universal principles. However, the fabric of existence is vast and multifaceted, and many spiritual traditions affirm that we are not alone in this universe. Beyond the veil of the physical world, there exists a myriad of other consciousnesses—non-corporeal beings at various levels of evolution and intention. And it is here that the dynamics of pacts take on an added complexity: when the agreement is not merely a unilateral declaration but involves, whether intentionally or not, one of these spiritual entities.

The spectrum of these consciousnesses is immense, ranging from the luminous figures of religious faith to the darker denizens of legends and folklore. In the popular imagination, the idea of a pact often evokes dramatic images of Faustian bargains, where desperate or ambitious individuals trade their souls with dark beings in exchange for earthly power, wealth, or forbidden knowledge. Although such archetypes exist in the collective unconscious and may represent extreme cases, interactions with spiritual entities through promises and agreements can occur in far more ordinary and subtle ways. Consider the devout person who, before a sacred image, promises a patron saint a specific offering or a change of life in exchange for an urgent grace. Or the individual who, during meditation or a dream, feels the presence of a spiritual guide and vows to follow certain instructions if granted assistance at a crossroads in life. Even the act of asking for protection from a deceased ancestor, promising to honor their memory in a particular way, may be seen as establishing an agreement with a non-physical consciousness. In all these cases, the commitment transcends the individual self and comes to involve another intelligence, another being within the invisible universe.

The fundamental implication of this is that the energetic bond created by the pact is not limited to connecting the person to the idea or content of the promise. It establishes a direct link, a channel of communication and influence, with the specific spiritual consciousness that was invoked or that agreed to participate in the agreement. A relationship is thus formed, even if tenuous or not consciously recognized, governed by the implicit or explicit terms of the pact. However, the dynamics of this relationship may vary greatly depending on the nature and evolutionary level of the entity involved.

Let us first consider interactions with entities perceived as benevolent—spiritual mentors, guardian angels, intercessory saints, loving ancestors. When an agreement is made with such consciousnesses, the spiritualist perspective suggests that their response will be guided by love, wisdom, and respect for the individual's free will. A luminous entity may indeed inspire and encourage the person to fulfill their promise, especially if the commitment aligns with the greater good and the evolution of the soul. It may send signs, intuitions, or facilitate circumstances that aid in honoring the vow. However, it is unlikely to exert coercion, impose its will, or actively punish failure to comply. Its role would be more that of a patient guide, understanding human difficulties and always pointing toward the path of growth, even if that means learning from the failure to honor the commitment. Any "collection" of the debt, if it occurs, would be more like a loving reminder from the soul itself regarding its original intention.

On the other hand, the scenario can be quite different when dealing with entities of a lower nature, more self-serving, or even overtly malicious. The invisible universe, like the visible one, contains beings with varying degrees of consciousness and ethics. A selfish entity, or one attached to its own interests, may view a pact as a strictly commercial contract, an agreement to be fulfilled to the letter. Should the person fail to deliver their part of the bargain, the entity may feel entitled to "actively collect" the debt. This collection can manifest in disturbing ways: negative mental influences, obsessive thoughts related to the pact, the creation of obstacles in the person's life, persistent misfortune, or even energetic attacks aimed at weakening or destabilizing the individual until they "pay" what is owed, according to the entity's interpretation. In such cases, the pact becomes a trap, a bond that imprisons rather than liberates.

In more serious situations, especially in pacts made with dark intentions, out of ignorance of the risks, or at moments of extreme vulnerability and despair, what is known as spiritual obsession may occur. Here, the entity involved in the pact not only seeks to collect the debt but attempts to establish a more direct control over the person's life and energy. It may manage to "attach itself to the individual's energetic field" like a subtle parasite, feeding on their vitality and deeply influencing their thoughts, emotions, and even physical health. The person may feel they are no longer in control of themselves, hear intrusive voices, suffer from recurring nightmares, or experience a series of misfortunes that seem to go beyond mere coincidence. Spiritual obsession is a serious consequence that highlights the dangers of engaging in careless or unhealthy agreements with unknown forces from the invisible plane.

All of this converges toward an important conclusion: dealing with pacts that involve other spiritual consciousnesses requires heightened attention and responsibility. The dynamics become more complex, for we are no longer dealing solely with our own energy and psychology but also with the will and nature of another being. Discernment becomes absolutely crucial—to strive to understand, as much as possible, with whom or what one is establishing a commitment. Blind faith or desperate promises made to any force that seems to listen may open unwanted doors.

It is at this point that self-knowledge and spiritual maturity prove not merely desirable but essential. The individual who seeks to establish an alliance with an entity, whether luminous or of more ambiguous origin, must first examine their own motivations with honesty. What is being offered? What is expected in return? Is there a true understanding of the nature of the bond being proposed? Often, the desire for immediate relief or the craving for answers leads to rash decisions, to the symbolic signing of agreements whose price will later be charged with spiritual interest. For this reason, practices such as meditation, reflective prayer, consultation with ethical masters, or reliance on trustworthy traditions can be powerful allies when deciding whether a pact should, in fact, be made—and, if so, under what conditions and with what safeguards.

This cautious approach, however, should not be confused with fear or paranoia. Relationships with spiritual entities, when based on lucidity, integrity, and elevated intention, can bring significant contributions to one's personal path. A pact need not be a prison: it can become an instrument of alignment with deeper purposes, a kind of renewal of vows with one's own soul, now in dialogue with other intelligences of the cosmos. In these cases, the commitment functions as a sacred bridge, a link of cooperation between dimensions, nourished by mutual trust and respect for free will. Even so, even under these ideal conditions, the commitment must be continually reassessed in light of inner evolution. What seemed fair yesterday may today appear limited or unnecessary. Flexibility and humility in the face of one's own journey are as fundamental as the courage to take on a promise.

Ultimately, the relationship with spiritual entities through pacts is a powerful path, but one that must be walked with steady feet and an awakened heart. The invisible is not, by definition, evil or good—it is, above all, a field of possibilities and a reflection of the very consciousness that accesses it. Knowing whom one speaks to, what is promised, and why it is promised is part of a spiritual ethic that protects, guides, and strengthens. In this balance between reverence and discernment, the human being finds not only the necessary safety for their choices but also the wisdom to walk between worlds without losing sight of the integrity of their own spirit.

Chapter 12
Subtle Energies

Our exploration of pacts has led us to consider agreements made with other consciousnesses—spiritual entities inhabiting invisible dimensions. This interaction adds a relational layer of complexity to our commitments. However, the panorama of energetic bonds that we can create through pledged words is even broader. Not every pact or solemn vow necessarily involves a "someone" on the other side—a personalized entity with whom we establish dialogue or exchange. Quite often, the commitment is directed toward more abstract forces, elevated principles, fervently embraced ideals, or even collective energy fields generated by humanity itself. These subtle energies, though impersonal, can acquire considerable strength and exert a profound, binding influence on those who dedicate themselves to them.

Consider the great ideals that drive history and inspire human action. A person, moved by a deep sense of righteousness, may make a solemn vow to dedicate their life to fighting for Justice, no matter the cost. Another, passionate in the pursuit of knowledge, may swear eternal loyalty to Truth, committing never to stray from it, even at the expense of personal sacrifice. An artist may consecrate their existence to Beauty, an activist to Freedom, a mystic to unconditionally serving the Light against the perceived Darkness in the world. In all these cases, the vow is not made to a specific person or spirit, but to a concept, to an abstract principle that, for the individual, assumes an almost divine importance. The counterpart of the pact here is a force-idea, an archetypal energy representing that elevated value. Similarly, one may devote their entire life to a political ideology or a social movement, swearing unwavering loyalty to the cause, seeing it as the highest expression of their values.

Although these ideals and principles do not possess individualized consciousness like a spiritual entity, they are not energetically neutral. When large numbers of people invest thoughts, emotions, and actions into a particular ideal or belief, this collective energy can coalesce, forming what some esoteric traditions call an *egregore*. An *egregore* is essentially an autonomous field of psychic energy, created and sustained by the shared faith and devotion of a group. Religions, initiatic orders, intense political movements, and even large corporations with strong internal cultures can generate powerful *egregores*. These subtle energetic structures develop a kind of "life of their own," possessing a characteristic vibration, implicit operating rules, and a tendency to perpetuate themselves and influence their members.

When a person makes a vow or oath before an *egregore*, or dedicates their life to an ideal strongly associated with one, they establish a direct connection between their personal energetic field and that collective energy field. They attune to the vibrational frequency of the *egregore* and come under its influence. The beliefs, values, emotions, and even biases shared by the group may begin to subtly permeate the individual's perceptions and choices, often without their conscious awareness. The *egregore* can offer a sense of belonging, strength, and purpose, but it can also demand conformity and loyalty.

Herein lie the challenges, especially when, over time, the individual begins to evolve in their own beliefs and question the dogmas or practices associated with the ideal or group to which they are bound. Attempting to diverge from the path outlined by the *egregore* or to break the vow made to that principle may generate painful internal conflict and a sense of energetic resistance. The person may feel inexplicably drained, as though their vital energy is being pulled back into the collective field they are trying to leave behind. They may experience a constant inner struggle, a sense of betrayal or guilt for no longer being able to align with the original commitment. It is as if the very energy of the ideal or the *egregore*—that subtle yet powerful force—pulls them back, resisting their attempt at individuation or change of course. The energetic loyalty established by the vow creates an inertia that is difficult to overcome.

Many organizations, especially those of initiatic or religious nature, intuitively or explicitly understand this mechanism. The requirement of vows of obedience, secrecy, or lifelong dedication is not merely a symbolic formality. It is a deliberate psychomagical technique to energetically bind members to the group's *egregore*, thereby ensuring cohesion, loyalty, and the continuity of the organization. The vow functions as a portal that connects the individual to the reservoir of collective energy, strengthening both the member and the *egregore* itself, while also creating a bond that may be difficult to sever should the person wish to follow a different path in the future.

Thus, the landscape of pacts and vows is broader than we might initially suppose. Our solemn commitments can connect us not only to conscious spiritual entities but also to these streams of subtle energy—these impersonal force fields generated by collective ideals and beliefs. Recognizing this dimension is crucial for those who seek spiritual freedom. The limitations or conflicts we experience may not stem from an agreement with a specific being but from an energetic entanglement with a force-idea or an *egregore* to which we once pledged fidelity.

This understanding radically expands the field of self-reflection, inviting the individual to look beyond visible figures and revered names to perceive what invisible forces their soul has committed to over the course of life—and possibly, over many lives. When we feel trapped by behaviors, beliefs, or loyalties that no longer resonate with our present truth, an ancient bond with an *egregore* or ideal that once gave meaning but now restricts may be at play. This recognition should not be a cause for guilt but for clarity: honoring the path traveled is important, but recognizing the moment to release certain bonds is a sign of spiritual maturity. Blind loyalty to ideas that no longer fit our inner expansion can block the flow of evolution and obscure the perception of what is newly calling us.

Breaking with an *egregore* or ideal that no longer serves our growth does not necessarily mean denying its past importance. It means understanding that every vow, even the noblest, must remain alive, dynamic, in constant dialogue with present consciousness. The energy once nourished with devotion can—and should—be redirected if the soul's higher purpose so demands. In this process, it may be necessary to engage in release rituals, silent internal ceremonies of disengagement, or practices that dissolve the vibrational entanglement. The liberation from a subtle pact does not occur solely on the plane of ideas but also in the energetic field where the true power of these commitments resides. The act of closing a cycle of loyalty to an *egregore* requires both courage and reverence—it is, in itself, a new pact with the freedom to be.

By recognizing the role of subtle energies in our journey, we make room to assume greater conscious authorship over that to which we choose to bind ourselves. Spiritual freedom is not achieved by rejecting all bonds but by lucidly choosing those that resonate with our deepest truth. Vows and pacts are not necessarily prisons; they can be bridges of light, provided they are made with awareness and reviewed with honesty over time. In this delicate balance between commitment and freedom, between loyalty and renewal, the human being finds not only a path of authenticity but also a safe way to relate to the invisible—whether it be inhabited by conscious entities or collective forces that shape the destiny of the soul.

Chapter 13
Spiritual Contracts

Our exploration of pacts, vows, and oaths has revealed an intricate universe of energetic commitments, ranging from desperate pleas to agreements with spiritual entities and alliances with abstract ideals. Each form carries its own nuance, its own binding force. Now, we are invited to broaden our perspective even further, to contemplate these commitments not as isolated events or mere biographical accidents, but as possible expressions of something deeper and more comprehensive: the soul's spiritual contracts. In this view, the pacts and vows we make throughout a lifetime may be understood as specific clauses, addendums, or activations within greater agreements that our spiritual essence assumes along its long evolutionary journey.

The concept of a spiritual contract transcends the idea of a promise made under pressure or a bargain struck with the divine. It encompasses the notion that the soul, in its wisdom and desire for growth, actively participates in the planning of its incarnational experiences. Many spiritual traditions propose the existence of a "soul contract"—a plan outlined prior to birth, in which the spirit, in consultation with guides or a higher consciousness, selects certain challenges, lessons, significant relationships, or missions of service to be experienced on Earth. These pre-incarnational choices function as sacred agreements, commitments voluntarily undertaken by the soul with itself and, at times, with other souls who will take part in this earthly dance. The purpose is not to predetermine every detail but to establish the main lines, central themes, and core lessons the soul intends to explore in that specific lifetime.

It is important to distinguish these pre-existing soul contracts from the pacts and vows we consciously (or desperately) make during life. Soul contracts are generally established from a higher perspective, with a panoramic view of the soul's evolutionary needs. Life pacts, on the other hand, tend to be responses to immediate circumstances, shaped by the emotions, beliefs, and limitations of the incarnated personality at that moment. However, though distinct in their origin and level of consciousness, both types of agreements exert a powerful influence on the course of life and personal destiny. They are not mutually exclusive; in fact, they often intertwine and influence one another.

A significant pact or vow made during life—such as a pledge of eternal love between two souls, a vow of dedication to a specific cause, or even a complex agreement with a spiritual entity—does not remain merely a feature of the current biography. It becomes integrated into the greater tapestry of the individual's spiritual contracts. It becomes an additional clause, a specification or modification of the original plan, with the potential to extend its influence beyond the present incarnation. The energy and intention invested in that earthly commitment are registered at the soul level and become part of its "contractual baggage," affecting future choices and experiences until the contract is fulfilled, renegotiated, or consciously dissolved. Thus, the acts of will and commitment made by the incarnated personality possess the power to actively shape the soul's spiritual contracts.

This interconnectedness leads us to a profound spiritual perspective: ultimately, nothing occurs by chance. If a person feels compelled to make a particularly strong vow or finds themselves involved in a situation that leads to a desperate pact, it may not be solely the result of external circumstances. There may have been an underlying soul contract—a spiritual predisposition to experience that specific type of learning related to responsibility, to the consequences of one's word, or to the central theme of the vow (such as poverty, loyalty, sacrifice, or forgiveness). The external situation may have served as the necessary trigger, attracted or co-created by the soul itself, to bring forth that contractual clause which required attention.

From this vantage point, even the experience of breaking a pact and facing its karmic and emotional consequences can be seen as an integral part of a greater spiritual contract. The soul may have chosen, at higher levels, to go through the entire cycle—the commitment, the failure, the resulting suffering, the quest for understanding, and finally, redemption and learning—as a way of mastering a particularly challenging lesson in integrity, free will, or compassion. What appears as painful failure on the surface may, in fact, be a crucial step in fulfilling a deeper evolutionary contract, carefully designed for the maximum growth of consciousness.

Embracing this broader perspective of spiritual contracts radically transforms our understanding of the pacts and promises that mark our journey. They cease to be isolated events, potentially frightening or sources of inescapable guilt, and become significant milestones in a continuous voyage of learning and self-discovery that extends across many lifetimes. Each commitment, whether honored or not, becomes an opportunity for learning—a clause in a greater curriculum aimed at our expansion and return to unity. This view does not diminish the seriousness or responsibility associated with our vows but places them within a context of purpose and meaning that transcends immediate drama.

Understanding our pacts and vows as part of larger spiritual contracts is also a fundamental step in preparing for the work of transformation and release. If they are contracts—even the oldest and deepest—there arises the possibility of reviewing them, renegotiating their terms in light of our current consciousness, or consciously declaring their completion once the lesson has been learned. The soul is not irreversibly bound to past agreements, especially those made in ignorance or desperation. By assuming our spiritual sovereignty and our capacity to co-create our reality, we can begin to interact consciously with these contracts, seeking to align our commitments with our highest good and present evolutionary purpose.

This possibility of consciously revisiting spiritual contracts invites us to adopt an active stance toward our own spiritual history. It is not a matter of denying old commitments, but of shedding light on them, understanding what still serves and what has already fulfilled its purpose. This process requires inner listening, emotional courage, and often the support of practices that facilitate contact with the deeper levels of being—such as therapeutic regressions, journeys of self-knowledge, release rituals, or guided meditations focused on spiritual clarity. As we revisit our alliances with a more mature consciousness, we gain the opportunity to update, redirect, or conclude them with gratitude and respect, avoiding both stagnation and energetic conflict with the new phases of our journey.

Many of the seemingly inexplicable challenges we face may be rooted in still-active spiritual contracts whose clauses have not been revisited since they were established—whether in previous lives or in this very existence. The repetition of patterns, the sense of persistent blockages, the feeling of being bound to a mission or relationship that has lost its meaning—all of these may signal that spiritual agreements are calling for review. When we approach these roots with compassion and discernment, we create space for new contracts to be written—now in full alignment with the expanded consciousness we have cultivated. The soul, after all, is not a prisoner of its past; it is the living author of its evolution, capable of adjusting its course as it grows in wisdom and love.

By understanding spiritual contracts as guiding threads of our incarnational experience, we access a more integrated view of life. Nothing is irrelevant, no vow too small, no rupture the end. Everything weaves together in a continuous movement of refinement and integration. Each pact made or dissolved is a step in the soul's learning about the power of intention, the responsibility of choice, and the beauty of conscious commitment. On this path, we are called to live with greater presence, to choose with greater clarity, and to honor not only the agreements of the past but, above all, those we make now—with ourselves, with others, and with the greater mystery that guides us toward our true purpose.

Chapter 14
Hidden Influence

As we come to understand pacts, vows, and oaths as potential clauses within broader spiritual contracts, woven throughout our soul's journey, a pressing question arises: how do these ancient soul agreements—commitments made in times long past or in moments of intensity within this very life—manifest concretely in our daily experience? If they do indeed persist as invisible bonds or energetic programs, how does their subtle yet tenacious presence shape our choices, emotions, and the circumstances we encounter? It is here that we turn our attention to the hidden influence of these agreements, to the ways in which they operate beneath the surface of consciousness, acting like subterranean currents that may redirect the course of our personal river without our awareness of their guiding force.

Many of the recurring difficulties, the negative patterns that seem to pursue us, or the limitations that frustrate us despite our best efforts, may have their deepest roots in these invisible contracts and pacts. Their influence is rarely obvious or dramatic; it does not announce itself with fanfare or present as a visible chain. On the contrary, its operation is subtle, persistent, resembling a computer program running silently in the background. It is not on the main screen, it does not draw attention to itself, yet it consumes resources, affects performance, and may even redirect commands unexpectedly. In much the same way, an ancient vow or pact operates in the subconscious layers of the mind and soul, coloring perceptions, influencing decisions, and keeping certain energetic frequencies active without the current personality being aware of the process.

It is both fascinating and at times unsettling to observe how, without realizing it, a person's decisions and reactions may be consistently shaped by a forgotten commitment. Take, for example, someone who, in a past life or perhaps during a passionate romance in their youth, swore eternal love to another soul, perhaps just before a tragic separation. In their present life, this person may feel a deep longing for a relationship, but unconsciously compares every new partner to the idealized image of that ancient love, finding flaws in everyone and perpetuating their solitude. Or, alternatively, they may meet a promising partner but begin to sabotage the relationship as it deepens—starting arguments, withdrawing emotionally—as if a part of them must remain "faithful" to that primordial vow, even at the cost of present happiness. The person may rationalize their behavior in many ways, but the hidden driving force is unconscious loyalty to the past pact.

Consider another case: someone who, perhaps in a previous lifetime as a monk or through a promise made during an act of extreme religious devotion, took a vow of obedience or silence. In this life, that person may struggle immensely to express their opinions, to defend their rights, to assume leadership roles, or simply to say "no." They may feel paralyzing anxiety when confronting authority or needing to assert themselves, even in situations where it would be perfectly reasonable to do so. Consciously, they may desire to be more assertive, yet an internal force seems to block them—a remnant of that old program of submission or self-denial, whose origin they do not consciously know. The same principle applies to vows of poverty, which may result in chronic financial self-sabotage, or vows of sacrifice, which may manifest as an inability to care for one's own needs.

The central idea that emerges from these examples is both disturbing and liberating: though we may see no physical chains binding us, forces from the past are still active in the present. Psychic energies, crystallized intention patterns, soul loyalties—all operate from an invisible dimension, yet with very tangible effects in our three-dimensional reality. Our lives may be subtly guided by decisions made long ago, in completely different contexts, by versions of ourselves we no longer recognize. This realization may initially create discomfort—a sense that we are not entirely masters of our own destiny. Yet it also offers a powerful key for understanding and change.

This is the moment to invite the reader to become a detective of their own life, an attentive observer of the hidden currents that may be at work. Begin to pay attention, with curiosity and without judgment, to those aspects of your life that seem resistant to all attempts at change. Observe situations that frustratingly repeat themselves—in relationships, career, finances, or health. Note the limitations that seem to have no logical cause or proportion to your efforts. Investigate those internal impulses that seem to act against your own interests, those moments of self-sabotage that arise just as you are about to achieve a desired goal. Record recurring dreams, pay attention to feelings or reactions that seem disproportionate to current circumstances. These may be valuable clues—smoke signals indicating the presence of a hidden fire, the influence of an old pact or contract operating in the shadows.

Awakening to the possibility of the hidden influence of pacts is a crucial step. It shifts us from being passive victims of circumstance to becoming active investigators of our own inner reality. As we begin to suspect that certain challenges may have deeper origins linked to these spiritual commitments, a new motivation arises: the desire to unravel these mysteries, to bring these hidden conditionings into the light, and ultimately, to resolve them. The awareness of this invisible influence ignites the flame of hope that real change is possible—not through futile battles against windmills, but through identifying and dissolving the true causes that hold us back.

However, the investigation of these hidden bonds should not be driven by a reflex of rejection or by a rush to break free from anything that appears limiting. Often, the very impulse to "break away" can reinforce the ties we wish to dissolve, especially if it is fueled by judgment, anger, or denial. The key lies in approaching these pacts with a broader perspective, recognizing the role they have played in our journey thus far. After all, even the vows that now seem to restrict us were originally sincere attempts to protect, to love, to serve, or to evolve. Looking upon them with compassion is essential for integrating and transforming them. The healing of these commitments does not occur through force or repression, but through understanding and transmutation. The process may be assisted by practices such as family constellations, conscious regressions, therapeutic writing, or guided meditations focused on releasing ancestral and karmic patterns.

As light is brought to these ancient pacts, one begins to reclaim personal power at levels previously inaccessible. The same channels that once served as conduits for unconscious influence can be requalified as pathways for a more authentic expression of the soul. What previously operated as a silent limitation may become a source of wisdom, once its origin and motivation are understood. In many cases, it is not necessary to "erase" the pact but to reframe it: transforming a vow of silence into a commitment to compassionate listening and conscious speech; a vow of poverty into a new relationship with detachment and responsible abundance; a pledge of eternal fidelity into a present, free, and renewed love. Thus, the energy that once imprisoned becomes creative momentum, and the old contracts become platforms for growth.

Revealing the hidden influence of pacts is, therefore, more than an exercise in self-knowledge—it is an act of spiritual sovereignty. By becoming aware of these invisible forces and recognizing them with maturity, we begin to write, with greater clarity, the new agreements that will shape our future experience. Life ceases to be a repetition of inherited patterns and becomes a work co-created between our deepest essence and the purpose we now choose to fulfill. This is true empowerment: realizing that even the oldest and most subtle bonds hold no greater power than the awakened consciousness that chooses, with courage, to live in coherence with its own truth.

Chapter 15
Repetitive Patterns

The hidden influence of spiritual pacts and contracts, that invisible force operating behind the scenes of the psyche, rarely remains completely concealed. Like an underground current that eventually surfaces in springs or marshy areas, the energy of these ancient commitments often manifests in tangible and observable ways in our daily lives through repetitive patterns. These are the cycles of events, relational dynamics, and recurring obstacles that stubbornly return no matter how much we try to change course. Naming and identifying these patterns is a crucial step toward bringing the hidden influence of the past into the light of consciousness, transforming what once seemed like an immutable fate into a puzzle to be solved.

When we speak of repetitive patterns in this context, we are not referring merely to simple behavioral habits, like nail-biting or procrastination. We refer to larger sequences of events, life scripts that seem to play out on a loop. Romantic relationships that start with great intensity but invariably end in the same painful way, with the same types of conflicts or betrayals. Careers that promise success but repeatedly face insurmountable obstacles at the last moment, leading to failure or stagnation. Financial cycles where periods of gain are always followed by unexpected losses, keeping the person trapped in constant material insecurity. Or even emotional patterns, like waves of deep sadness or overwhelming anxiety that arise cyclically without any apparent external cause. It's the unsettling feeling of reliving the same movie, with slight variations in setting and characters, but the same fundamental plot and frustrating outcome.

But why do these patterns repeat so insistently? If an ancient pact or vow is active, how does it orchestrate these repetitions? The key lies in the nature of unresolved energy. As we have seen, a broken commitment or a karmic lesson associated with a pact leaves a "loose end," an energetic imbalance within the soul's field. This unresolved energy functions as a subtle magnet, attracting or co-creating circumstances that resonate with the central theme of the original commitment. The active spiritual bond with the past vow continues to emit a specific frequency, and the law of cause and effect, in its educational role, tends to mirror that frequency back in the form of concrete experiences. Repetition is not a punishment but a persistent call from the soul and the universe to face that unresolved issue, to finally learn the lesson contained within or to find a way to release or honor the old agreement. Each repetition of the pattern is essentially a new opportunity offered for healing and integration.

Let us consider some examples to illustrate how this might unfold. Imagine someone who, in a past life or in a moment of youthful fervor, swore unconditional loyalty and sacrifice to a particular cause or person. This energy of self-denial and selfless service may still be active. In their current life, this person may repeatedly find themselves in situations where their own boundaries are disregarded, where they feel compelled to prioritize others' needs over their own, whether at work, in the family, or in romantic relationships. They may even attempt to change, to set boundaries, but invariably fall back into the same pattern of overgiving, later feeling resentful and exhausted. The external scenario changes, but the internal script of sacrifice, dictated by the old spiritual bond, continues to repeat.

Or consider the person who, after a particularly traumatic experience of betrayal, vowed to themselves with all the strength of their pain: "I will never trust anyone again; I will never open myself to love." This vow, born of hurt, can become a powerful subconscious program. In the present life, they may deeply desire a safe and intimate relationship but continually attract partners who confirm their original belief: individuals who are emotionally unavailable, afraid of commitment, or who ultimately betray their trust in some way. The pattern of loneliness or superficial and painful relationships repeats, not because they are unlucky or unworthy of love, but because the energy of the old vow continues to operate, filtering their perceptions and attracting experiences that validate the decision to keep their heart closed.

This is the moment to turn inward, with honesty and courage. Ask yourself the uncomfortable but potentially revealing question: What events or emotions in my life feel like a recurring movie? In which areas do I feel trapped in a vicious cycle, running in circles without moving forward? Analyze your relationships: is there a specific type of person you repeatedly attract? Do the conflicts or reasons for breakups tend to be similar? Observe your financial life: are there recurring patterns of scarcity, debt, or loss? In your career, do you face the same types of obstacles or frustrations across different jobs? In your health, do certain symptoms or vulnerabilities appear cyclically? Allow yourself to recognize these loops without judgment, simply as a neutral observer gathering data about your own existence.

Identifying a clear and persistent pattern is like finding the loose end of a tangled ball of yarn. This repetitive pattern becomes a valuable guiding thread. By following this thread attentively—through self-analysis, meditation, intuition, or perhaps with the help of therapies that access deeper memories—we can eventually reach the source of the entanglement, the initial knot: the pact, vow, or oath that gave rise to that cycle. The pattern ceases to be an indecipherable enigma and reveals a potential root cause.

It is crucial at this point to abandon the idea that these patterns are mere coincidences, the result of bad luck, or unchangeable personality traits. Such a perspective keeps us powerless. Instead, the invitation is to seriously consider the possibility that they are significant signs, encoded messages from our own soul or the universe, pointing to unlearned lessons or agreements still active on the subtle plane. They are symptoms of a deeper cause that needs to be discovered and addressed.

Recognizing your own repetitive patterns is, therefore, a giant step on the path to liberation. It is the moment when the hidden influence begins to lose its power because it is no longer hidden. Consciousness transforms the unconscious cycle into a matter to be resolved. Although the solution may require further work and exploration, the simple act of identifying the pattern and suspecting its link to a past commitment already fundamentally alters the dynamic. One ceases to be a passive victim of repetition and becomes an active agent in the quest to break the cycle.

This transition from passivity to conscious action does not happen instantly but is marked by a series of small awakenings, flashes of clarity that gradually integrate into daily life. A recognized pattern is like a forgotten word that returns to the tongue: it begins to sound familiar, to make sense, and gradually allows us to name what was previously a vague sensation. By naming, we define; by defining, we gain freedom. This is the key that transforms the repetitive pattern from an implacable destiny into an ongoing lesson. And by adopting this perspective, we come to see that these cycles are not enemies but persistent teachers, insistent on teaching us what we may have ignored for lifetimes. In this context, suffering is not punishment but the soul's loving insistence that we look where we have avoided looking.

This process of revelation requires sensitivity but also commitment. As patterns become visible, the temptation may arise to fall into regret or harsh self-criticism: "How did I not see this before?" "Why did I repeat this mistake so many times?" But it is essential to understand that learning is only possible when consciousness is ready. Each repeated cycle was not in vain; it prepared the ground for the present awakening. True transformation occurs when, upon recognizing the pattern, we stop fighting against it and begin to dialogue with its origin. We can ask: what part of me believed I needed to live this? What value or wound was behind this pact? What did I gain, even unconsciously, by maintaining this cycle? These questions do not seek blame but understanding. And it is this understanding that dissolves the pattern at its root.

Breaking free from a repetitive pattern does not necessarily mean erasing its traces from life. Often, they continue to appear but no longer carry the same weight, the same inevitability. They become echoes, not commands. And it is at this point that we realize that the power has always been within us—not in the sense of absolute control, but of transformative presence. The cycle loses strength because consciousness has gained depth. And thus, step by step, the ancient pacts are undone, not with denial but with maturity, gratitude, and the renewed choice to live with greater truth. By recognizing, investigating, and transforming the cycle, we create space for something new to be born: a life no longer governed by what was, but by the freedom to be what is now understood.

Chapter 16
Self-Sabotage

The patterns that repeat in our lives, like insistent echoes of an unresolved past, are perhaps the most evident signs of the hidden influence of ancient pacts and vows. However, this influence can manifest in an even more disconcerting and painful way: self-sabotage. We speak of that often inexplicable tendency to act against our own interests, to undermine our most cherished goals precisely when they seem within reach. The person consciously desires prosperity, love, success, health, yet somehow their own behaviors and choices seem to conspire to prevent these desires from being fulfilled. While psychology offers various explanations for the mechanisms of self-sabotage, the spiritual perspective invites us to consider an additional layer: the possibility that this self-destructive conduct is not merely a psychological conflict, but the result of an internal contradictory force, fueled by the lingering energy of an old, unreleased commitment.

Picture the inner scene: on one side, the conscious will, the legitimate desire for a fuller, happier life; on the other, a hidden force, an invisible loyalty to a past decree, pulling in the opposite direction. This internal contradiction does not operate out of malice, but out of a kind of distorted integrity, a fidelity to the original program established by the pact or vow. If, in the past, the soul solemnly committed to renunciation, solitude, or sacrifice, part of it may still feel obligated to honor that commitment, even if the present personality yearns for abundance, connection, and self-realization. Self-sabotage then emerges as the result of this internal tug-of-war, where unconscious actions seek to maintain coherence with the old vow, frustrating the conscious desires of the present.

Let us consider concrete examples of this dynamic. Imagine someone who, perhaps in a past life as a member of an ascetic religious order, or even in this life during a moment of intense devotion or guilt, made a sincere vow of poverty or extreme humility. Consciously, this person may now strive for financial stability, work hard, and pursue opportunities for growth. Yet whenever a real chance for significant gain or recognition arises—a major promotion, a promising investment, a lucrative project—something happens. The person may procrastinate on crucial decisions until the opportunity is lost, may make inexplicable mistakes that jeopardize the outcome, may suddenly feel unworthy or guilty for desiring more, and ultimately relinquish the chance. Externally, this may appear as bad luck or incompetence, but internally, it is the force of the old vow at work, ensuring that the person remains aligned with the energy of scarcity or self-imposed humility they once promised to uphold.

Likewise, consider someone who, after suffering a devastating romantic betrayal, swore solemnly in their pain: "I will never fall in love again; I will never allow anyone to hurt me like that." Years later, this person may feel deep loneliness and sincerely wish to find a loving and trustworthy partner. They may even meet someone who meets these desires, enter a promising relationship, and sense happiness on the horizon. And then, inexplicably, they begin to sabotage everything. They start to find insignificant faults in their partner, create conflicts over trivial matters, close off emotionally, and push the loved one away. Why? Because a part of them, still loyal to that vow made in pain, feels that falling in love again would be breaking their word, exposing them to the same vulnerability they vowed to avoid. Self-sabotage becomes the unconscious mechanism for keeping the heart "safe," closed, in compliance with the old decree of self-protection, even if it means perpetuating the loneliness that the conscious self so deeply laments.

It is essential, when contemplating these scenarios, to move away from the notion that self-sabotage necessarily implies a lack of ability, intelligence, or worthiness. The person who undermines their financial success may be highly capable and hardworking. The person who ruins promising relationships may be deeply loving and deserving of love. The problem does not lie in an inherent personal flaw, but rather in this deeply rooted loyalty conflict, this internal division between present desire and past pact. Recognizing this is crucial for self-compassion. It is not about blaming oneself for being unable to achieve what one desires, but about understanding that there may be a powerful, ancient energetic force acting in opposition to conscious goals.

Identifying this internal conflict is the key to beginning its dismantling. Self-sabotage, seen in this light, ceases to be irrational or shameful behavior and becomes a symptom, a valuable clue pointing to a possible unresolved bond. The invitation, then, is to engage in attentive and compassionate self-observation. Begin to notice those moments when you seem to "shoot yourself in the foot," especially when things were going well. When a promising opportunity arises, observe whether an internal resistance appears, a desire to procrastinate, a series of "mistakes," or a sudden loss of interest. When a relationship flourishes, notice whether you start to find faults, create distance, or feel inexplicable anxiety. Ask yourself: "What is this part of me that is sabotaging trying to protect or honor? To which old commitment might it still be loyal?"

Bringing these dynamics into the light of consciousness is the first step toward liberation. By understanding that self-sabotage may be the manifestation of an ancient pact, you begin to strip this unconscious mechanism of its power. You realize you are not doomed to repeat these self-destructive patterns. There is a cause, and where there is a cause, there can be a solution. This awareness prepares the ground for deeper work in specifically identifying the vow or pact in question and applying techniques for release and integration. The ultimate goal is to dissolve the internal conflict, release the energy trapped in the old commitment, and finally align conscious desire, action, and energetic flow toward the positive fulfillment and full life you long for and deserve.

When this old pact is finally brought to light and acknowledged, space is created for the full restoration of free will. The person, now aware of the spiritual root of their self-sabotage, can deliberately choose a new internal stance, a new narrative for their life. It is not a matter of fighting against the sabotaging part but of listening to it with respect, acknowledging its reasons, and showing it that times have changed, that current conditions no longer require the same sacrifice. This compassionate inner dialogue marks the beginning of reconciliation between the divided parts, fostering a reintegration of the psyche that has long been at war with itself.

As this reconciliation unfolds, new behaviors begin to emerge naturally. Procrastination gives way to decisive action; the fear of being seen and recognized transforms into a desire to share one's gifts with the world; the fear of love opens up to trust in the present. The old vow need not be violently rejected but transformed through understanding and forgiveness. Certain spiritual practices, such as symbolic rituals of vow revocation, guided meditations, or soul retrieval therapies, can be extremely effective in this process. More than erasing the past, the aim is to integrate its lesson, releasing the trapped energy and converting it into vital force available for the creation of a new reality.

It is at this point that the cycle closes with purpose: when the force that once served pain is transformed into wisdom in service of healing. Self-sabotage ceases to be a dark obstacle and becomes a revealing path, leading to a reunion with inner truth and the inalienable right to live fully. Freeing oneself from these hidden pacts is to allow the soul to choose, with consciousness and freedom, new paths—paths of harmony, prosperity, and love.

Chapter 17
Emotional Blockages

The insidious influence of unresolved pacts and vows extends beyond repetitive patterns of events and the self-sabotaging behaviors that undermine our goals. It penetrates even deeper, reaching the core of our sensitive experience—the delicate ecosystem of our heart and mind. There, in the inner landscapes where our feelings are born and flow, these ancient commitments can erect invisible barriers, create dams in the natural flow of emotions, and generate deep blockages that prevent us from feeling and expressing the fullness of our being. Many persistent negative emotions, which seem to defy logical or circumstantial explanation, may have their roots embedded in these forgotten or unresolved spiritual bonds.

How often do we find ourselves engulfed in a diffuse sadness that hovers over us without any apparent reason, a melancholy that shades sunny days with tones of gray? Or experience irrational fears in situations that present no real danger—phobias that paralyze and limit our choices? Perhaps we carry a chronic difficulty in trusting others, even those who prove themselves trustworthy, or a corrosive distrust toward ourselves, our abilities, and our worth. These persistent emotional states, which resist conventional therapeutic approaches or efforts of positive thinking, may be signs of emotional blockages whose origins lie in an ancient pact or vow.

As we have seen, the energy of an unresolved commitment remains active within the subtle field. This energy carries a specific vibrational frequency, and this frequency can resonate with or generate corresponding emotional states. Take, for example, a vow to keep an eternal secret about a traumatic event or compromising information, perhaps made under threat or out of a distorted sense of loyalty. The energy of such a vow of silence may manifest in the present life as a persistent difficulty in communicating openly, expressing vulnerability, or establishing genuine intimacy. The person may feel emotionally constipated, unable to share their deepest feelings, as if an invisible gag were restraining them. The blockage does not reside in the throat but in the energetic field, sustained by the power of the old vow of secrecy.

Another poignant example is a vow of eternal loyalty to someone who has departed, either through death or separation. In the midst of grief, the person may have vowed never to love again, or promised to dedicate their life to keeping the memory of the loved one alive. While this promise may have offered temporary solace, its energy can create a lasting emotional blockage. The person may find themselves trapped in a perpetual sadness, an attachment to the past that prevents them from embracing new joys, new relationships, new possibilities for happiness in the present. The heart remains energetically bound to the one who has gone, and loyalty to the vow prevents openness to the new. The sadness becomes chronic, not merely as unprocessed grief, but as a state sustained by the force of the old commitment.

Even phobias or aversions that seem entirely irrational in light of one's current biography may sometimes be emotional echoes of traumatic events linked to pacts from past lives. An intense and inexplicable fear of water may trace back to a drowning that occurred after breaking a vow made aboard a ship. A paralyzing fear of heights may be tied to a fatal fall associated with a pledge made in a high place. A deep aversion to the idea of marriage, despite the conscious desire to form a family, may be the residue of a monastic vow or a disastrous marital experience tied to a pact in another existence. In these cases, the emotion (fear, aversion) acts as an anachronistic alarm, triggered by present stimuli that resonate with the original trauma where the pact was involved. The emotional blockage is the psychic scar of that ancient event.

These emotional blockages act like invisible walls erected around the heart and mind. They limit our ability to fully feel the spectrum of human emotions, to authentically connect with others and with life itself. They hinder the free expression of our inner truth and keep us partially imprisoned in the emotional landscape of the past, unable to inhabit the present with lightness and spontaneity. We live as though inside a fortress whose walls, though invisible, are painfully real in their limiting effects.

However, the very existence of these blockages, once recognized, can become a portal to clarity and healing. Upon noticing a persistent and seemingly causeless negative emotion, we can begin to inquire in a new way. Rather than simply trying to repress or fight the feeling, we can ask with curiosity and compassion: What is the deeper origin of this sadness, this fear, this distrust? What vow might my heart have made to remain so closed? What ancient commitment might my soul still be trying to honor through this limiting emotion? This loving investigation, this willingness to dialogue with our own difficult emotions, may begin to bring insights and dissolve the energetic foundations of the blockage.

It is essential in this process to welcome one's emotions, even the most uncomfortable ones. They are not enemies to be defeated but messengers carrying precious information about our deeper history. By allowing ourselves to feel what is present, without judgment, we create a safe space for memories or intuitions about the origins of these feelings to emerge. Each unexplained tear, each irrational shiver of fear, each wave of distrust may be a clue leading us back to the moment when a commitment was made—a thread that helps us unravel the emotional knot.

Understanding the link between emotional blockages and ancient pacts deepens our motivation to seek healing. We realize that we are not doomed to live under the yoke of these limiting emotions. They are symptoms of causes that can be understood and transformed. The work of releasing pacts thus becomes equally a work of emotional release, a process of dissolving the invisible walls and allowing the river of life and feeling to flow freely through us once again.

It is in this delicate process of recovery that the heart, once imprisoned by forgotten vows, begins to open to the possibility of a new pulse. As consciousness expands to recognize the subtle origins of the blockages, a kind of realignment begins: what once seemed like a senseless emotion now has context, a history, a root. And with this recognition comes the possibility of choice—not the automatic choice dictated by an invisible commitment, but the conscious choice to release, to forgive, to let go. Imprisoned emotions begin to find a voice, no longer as unconscious laments, but as legitimate expressions of a past that calls for resolution. Feeling once again becomes a source of connection rather than pain.

In this state of openness, emotional healing may take unexpected forms: revealing dreams, spontaneous memories, insights during meditation, or in simple everyday moments. Sometimes it is in the silence of contemplation that the soul whispers the truth of what needs to be released. Techniques such as intuitive writing, family constellations, conscious regression, or even artistic practices may serve as powerful vehicles for bringing repressed emotions to light, reinterpreting the pact, and finally dissolving the emotional armor. Each blockage overcome becomes a bridge to a richer, more connected experience—and the emotion, once contained, overflows into new ways of loving, creating, and living with presence.

As these inner locks dissolve, one begins to realize that feeling fully is not dangerous but essential. That living with an open heart is the true antidote to the pain of the past. And above all, that there is a loving wisdom behind every emotion, even those that once seemed overwhelming. The flow returns, and with it, the freedom to be whole once again.

Chapter 18
Life Limitations

The resonance of ancient pacts and vows is not confined to the inner landscapes of the mind and heart, manifesting as repetitive patterns, self-sabotage, or emotional blockages. Its hidden influence can overflow into the external world, crystallizing into concrete limitations that directly affect the most vital areas of our existence: our ability to prosper, our physical health, the quality of our relationships, and even our sense of purpose and direction in life. Often, it is precisely those most persistent impediments—those barriers that seem insurmountable despite all our efforts and the conventional solutions attempted—that may signal the presence of a limiting spiritual commitment operating in the shadows.

Let us observe the financial sphere. How many people struggle relentlessly to achieve stability or abundance, possess intelligence, talent, and work diligently, yet seem trapped in an endless cycle of scarcity? Money comes in but disappears inexplicably; promising opportunities vanish at the last minute; debts accumulate despite strict control. From a purely material or psychological perspective, such situations may be attributed to mismanagement, limiting beliefs about money, or simple bad luck. However, the spiritual perspective invites us to consider another possibility: the influence of an ancient vow of poverty or renunciation. Someone who, at some point in their soul's journey, swore to live in extreme simplicity or to renounce material possessions may carry this energetic signature with them. Their energy, even unconsciously, still resonates with the vibration of the "promised" scarcity, creating a subtle resistance to prosperity and attracting circumstances that maintain material difficulty, as if the soul were still trying to honor that old contract of detachment.

The area of health can also reflect these subtle dynamics. Of course, the vast majority of illnesses have well-established biological, environmental, or psychosomatic causes. However, in cases of chronic diseases that defy clear diagnoses, conditions that resist conventional treatments, or a persistent sense of low vitality without medical explanation, the possibility of energetic influences linked to pacts should not be dismissed. A vow of self-sacrifice, for instance—where one promised to "give their life" for a cause or for someone—may translate into a tendency to neglect one's own health or to exhaust one's vital energy. The energetic stress of an unresolved pact, especially one involving intense guilt or fear, may also, over time, affect the physical body, contributing to the onset or worsening of certain conditions. Or, as mentioned, an illness may be a karmic echo of traumatic events associated with a pact in past lives. Investigating these possibilities requires great discernment, but it may offer new perspectives where conventional medicine reaches its limits.

In relationships, the limitations imposed by ancient pacts may go beyond emotional blockages and manifest as a concrete inability to establish or sustain healthy bonds. A person may ardently desire a partner, actively seek one, yet encounter an emotional desert, or only attract superficial, abusive, or abruptly ending relationships. The sense of loneliness becomes a constant, a real limitation that defines their emotional experience. Behind this may lie the force of an eternal love vow made to another soul in a past life, a vow of celibacy, or a promise never to bond intimately again after great pain. The old commitment acts as an invisible barrier, preventing new meaningful connections from being established or flourishing, effectively keeping the person bound to the condition once promised.

Even our sense of purpose and professional path may be deeply affected. Someone who, in a moment of spiritual fervor, vowed to dedicate their life solely to God or to spiritual service may experience a painful internal conflict when attempting to follow a worldly career. They may encounter inexplicable failures, a lack of fulfillment, or a constant sense of being in the wrong place because part of them believes that only the originally promised spiritual vocation is legitimate and valid. Another person, perhaps bound to a vow of perpetual humility or invisibility, may struggle to claim their own worth, seek recognition for their talents, or attain positions of prominence, thus concretely limiting their professional and personal potential. The sensation of going in circles without finding clear direction in life may also sometimes be tied to restrictive vows preventing the soul from freely exploring its true potential.

It is also important to consider the possibility of limitations imposed by family pacts. Not every limiting bond was created by the individual in their current or past life. Perhaps an ancestor, under difficult circumstances, made a vow that, through unconscious family loyalty or energetic transmission across generations, continues to affect their descendants. Stories of families that seem "cursed" with poverty, specific illnesses, or repeated tragedies may, in some cases, have origins in an ancient pact. One example would be a vow made by a family group never to abandon their homeland, which could manifest in later generations as an inexplicable resistance or a series of failures whenever someone tries to move away in search of better opportunities, concretely limiting the life choices of their descendants.

What makes these limitations particularly frustrating is that they often do not yield to conventional solutions. The person may undergo therapy, seek financial counseling, follow medical treatments, change jobs—but the invisible barrier seems to persist. This occurs precisely because the root of the problem is not on the surface, but in that subtle bond, that energetic contract which ordinary approaches cannot access or dissolve.

Connecting these concrete life limitations to the possibility of underlying spiritual pacts or contracts offers a radical and hopeful shift in perspective. The difficulties cease to be seen as proof of personal incapacity, chronic bad luck, or cruel fate. They come to be viewed as possible effects of deeper causes, as symptoms of energetic agreements that, once identified, can be addressed. The transformative idea is that if these barriers are, in essence, contractual clauses, then contracts can be renegotiated, updated, or even terminated. This realization opens up a new horizon of possibilities, kindling hope for real and lasting change by addressing the spiritual and energetic roots of these limitations that can so severely restrict our life experience.

The next step is to courageously dive into this subtle and often nebulous territory where the records of these ancient commitments reside. It is an inner work that requires presence, honesty, and a willingness to review personal history from a new perspective—not as a succession of failures, but as a journey marked by invisible loyalties and forgotten contracts. The identification of these pacts may occur through spontaneous insights, deep therapeutic practices, or transformative spiritual experiences. As the individual recognizes that certain limitations no longer match their current desire for expansion and fulfillment, they are faced with the possibility of freeing themselves from these bonds with clarity, respect, and clear intention.

This process of release does not mean denying the value or original intention of the pact made in another time. On the contrary, recognizing it is a way of honoring it. Often, these commitments were made in a context of pain, faith, or extreme need, and understanding this with compassion is an essential part of healing. However, it is important to remember that the soul evolves, and what was once sacred may become obsolete. Breaking an old vow is not a betrayal of one's own history but a gesture of spiritual maturity: it is permission to live according to current consciousness, in harmony with the legitimate desires of the present. When this decision is made with clarity and integrity, it acts as a key that unlocks doors once sealed, allowing previously blocked opportunities to begin manifesting naturally.

Thus, life ceases to be a maze of frustrated attempts and becomes a fertile field of conscious creation. With the pacts dissolved, the energies once channeled into maintaining the old contract now serve the blossoming of the new. Health improves, professional paths expand, relationships become more authentic, and abundance begins to flow with less resistance. The soul, now freed from the invisible shackles of the past, regains its full capacity to choose, taking new steps toward a lighter, more coherent, and luminous existence.

Chapter 19
The Shadow of the Past

We have traveled a winding and at times dark path, exploring the nature of pacts, vows, and oaths—from the desperate cry that gives them birth to the intricate webs of consequences that unfold across energetic, karmic, emotional, and behavioral planes. We have seen how the power of spoken words can create invisible bonds, how these ties can stretch across lifetimes, how their rupture generates misalignments and spiritual debts, and how they manifest as repetitive patterns, self-sabotage, emotional blockages, and concrete limitations in our existence. Now, at the conclusion of this in-depth analysis of these commitments' effects, a synthesized image emerges—a powerful metaphor to encapsulate their persistent and often unconscious influence: the image of a shadow of the past that follows many of us.

This shadow is not made of the absence of light but of the substance of words once spoken and never released, of intentions crystallized that have lost their original purpose but not their energetic force. It is an ethereal presence, invisible to the eyes, yet often palpable to the soul's sensitivity. It follows us like a second silhouette, projected not by sunlight, but by the mass of our unresolved commitments, the stagnant energies of forgotten vows, and the karmic lessons still pending in relation to our given word. It is the accumulated baggage of spiritual agreements that, due to ignorance, fear, or inability, we have failed to honor or consciously dissolve.

What does it feel like to live under this shadow of the past? Often, it manifests as a diffuse yet constant sensation that there is something "unfinished." A subtle restlessness, a difficulty in fully relaxing, in feeling deep and lasting peace. It may feel like carrying a nameless weight, an invisible responsibility whose exact content escapes us, yet whose pressure we sense on our shoulders or in our hearts. It is a lack of lightness, a struggle to fully inhabit the joy of the present moment, as if part of us is always attentive to an unfinished task, to an unpaid debt somewhere in the vast ledger of the soul.

Even in life's happiest and brightest moments, this shadow can find a crack through which to slip in. A sudden wave of melancholy that arises without apparent reason in the midst of a celebration. A fleeting thought of unworthiness that crosses the mind upon receiving sincere praise. An inexplicable impulse toward self-sabotage that threatens to ruin a hard-earned achievement. These may be the whispers of the shadow, subtle reminders that there is an unresolved bond, an ancient loyalty that still claims a share of our energy and attention, preventing us from fully embracing happiness without reservation. The shadow acts as a subtle anchor, always ready to pull us back into the murkier waters of our past commitments.

Recognizing the potential existence of this shadow is a step of crucial importance—perhaps the most decisive one on the path to liberation. As long as we deny its presence, as long as we attribute all our difficulties solely to external factors or recent character flaws, we remain hopelessly bound to it. The shadow feeds on the unspoken, the unseen, the unacknowledged. It thrives in the darkness of our ignorance or refusal to look into the deeper layers of our soul's history. However, the moment we dare to confront the possibility that we are living under the effects of past spiritual decisions, something fundamental begins to shift.

In facing this possibility head-on, the shadow of the past starts to lose its frightening power. It ceases to be a threatening ghost, an unknown and uncontrollable force haunting us. It transforms into something that can be named, examined, understood. It comes to be seen not as a condemnation but as an integral part of our journey—a set of lessons and energies that need to be brought into the light, welcomed, and eventually transmuted. The shadow becomes a map that, while pointing to difficult territories, also indicates the way to hidden treasures of self-knowledge and healing. The fear of the unknown gives way to curiosity and a determination to illuminate these dark areas of our personal history.

This process of recognizing and accepting the possible influence of the shadow of the past serves as indispensable psychological preparation for the steps that follow. Having journeyed through the preceding chapters, the reader now holds a clearer understanding of what these pacts and vows are, how they are formed, how they operate through energetic and karmic mechanisms, and how they can subtly and concretely limit life. This diagnostic phase now comes to a close. The nature of the problem has been exposed in its various facets. The knowledge gained is not intended to instill fear or resignation but to empower through understanding.

With awareness awakened to the potential presence of this shadow and the mechanisms that sustain it, the motivation to seek the light of freedom naturally ignites. Once we understand how the chains hold us, we yearn to find the keys that can set us free. The journey now shifts from diagnosis to action, from understanding the problem to actively seeking the solution. The next steps will guide us through methods for identifying the specific signs of these pacts in our lives, accessing the memories that may reveal their origins, and finally, undertaking the processes of release and healing that will allow us to dissipate the shadow of the past and move toward a brighter, more authentic future.

This passage from recognition to liberation requires more than intellectual comprehension of what pacts are and their effects. It invites a sincere dive into the deepest layers of the soul, where the echoes of forgotten promises still vibrate—sometimes with unsuspected intensity. The true encounter with the shadow of the past occurs not when we study it from the outside but when we feel it from within—in the body, in the emotions, in the automatic gestures that stubbornly repeat old scripts. Healing begins when we stop seeing the shadow as something to fear or deny and start treating it as a legitimate part of our story—a part that merely asks to be heard, integrated, and ultimately released.

This type of acceptance is not a passive gesture but a radical act of spiritual responsibility. It means acknowledging that—even unconsciously—something within us once consented to form the bonds we now wish to undo. And in doing so, we also discover the power we have to rewrite those agreements. The commitment transforms: from a pact sealed by pain or ignorance, we move toward a new vow—the vow to live in alignment with the truth of the present, with the values that sustain us today, and with the love we wish to cultivate. The shadow, when traversed consciously, ceases to obscure the path and begins to reveal its latent light.

From this new clarity, we can finally turn our gaze to what lies ahead. The healing journey that now presents itself requires tools, practices, rituals, and above all, presence. If the path until now has been one of revelation and recognition, the next steps will be of conscious transformation. Armed with a deep understanding of the shadow and the pacts, we now walk not as victims of a hidden inheritance but as authors of a new narrative, ready to reclaim sovereignty over our spiritual destiny and to step lightly toward the wholeness that has always belonged to us.

Chapter 20
Signs of the Pact

The journey thus far has allowed us to grasp the profound nature of pacts and vows, the power they hold, and the many ways in which their often-hidden influence can shape our reality, projecting the shadow of the past onto our present. Recognizing this possibility is liberating in itself, as it removes us from the role of passive victims of unknown forces. Now, however, the investigation takes a crucial step forward: from a general understanding of the phenomenon to personal exploration. How can we identify, in our own lives, the concrete signs and clues that we may still be bound by these ancient commitments? Here begins the phase of becoming a detective of the soul—an invitation to scrutinize our experience with fresh eyes, attentive to the subtle hints that may reveal the presence of these spiritual ties.

The first step in this personal investigation is a guided self-analysis, a series of honest questions we can pose to ourselves. Set aside some quiet time, take a deep breath, and reflect without judgment on the following areas: Is there something in your life—perhaps a specific challenge or a persistent limitation—that seems absolutely impossible to change, no matter how much you try, no matter how many different strategies you apply? Do you feel, even vaguely, as if you once made a very important promise—something that demands your loyalty or effort—even though you cannot clearly recall what, when, or to whom you made that promise? Are there intense fears or recurring emotions in your life—perhaps deep sadness, specific anxiety, or difficulty in trusting—that seem disproportionate or inconsistent with your current life story, as if they belong to another script? Revisit the repetitive patterns you identified earlier: do they align with any of the archetypal themes of vows we discussed, such as poverty, loneliness, sacrifice, obedience, or vengeance? Is there any area in which you consistently self-sabotage, acting against your own conscious desires for happiness or success?

These questions are not meant to provide definitive answers but to activate your intuition and cellular memory, bringing to the surface potential areas of resonance with the theme of pacts.

Beyond direct introspection, the universe often sends us clues through synchronicities and revealing dreams. Pay attention to meaningful "coincidences." Have you repeatedly encountered references to a particular historical period, to a specific symbol (such as chains, contracts, religious robes, swords), or to the very theme of vows and oaths in books, films, conversations, or even in unexpected places? Such synchronistic occurrences may be nudges from your higher self or the universe, drawing your attention to something relevant in your soul's history. Similarly, dreams can serve as portals to the subconscious and deeper memories.

Recurrent dreams that transport you to past eras, that feature symbols of imprisonment or solemn commitments, or that evoke intense feelings of guilt, duty, or inexplicable loyalty, may be fragments of past-life memories where significant vows were made. Record these dreams, even the strangest or most fragmented ones, as they may hold valuable pieces of the puzzle.

Our everyday language may also carry unconscious echoes of these ancient commitments. Begin observing the habitual phrases, idiomatic expressions, or beliefs you verbalize frequently, especially in moments of difficulty or reflection. Do you often say things like: "Ah, this is my karma," "I must have done something to deserve this," "I feel like I carry a heavy burden," "A promise is a debt" (spoken with particular gravity), or "I'll never be rich/happy/loved"? These expressions, although often casually used in our culture, may in some cases be literal reflections of deeply rooted beliefs about spiritual debts or self-imposed limitations originating from past pacts. Paying attention to the words that leave your mouth can reveal much about the programs operating in your subconscious.

Perhaps one of the most powerful and direct signs is the intuitive and visceral response. Many people, when reading about pacts and vows or hearing stories that describe spiritual commitments—especially those made in dramatic circumstances or specific historical contexts—experience an immediate and inexplicable physical or emotional reaction. It might be a chill running down the spine, a sudden tightness in the chest, a wave of sadness or fear that arises without warning, or even a strong sense of déjà vu—a feeling of "I've been through this" or "this sounds strangely familiar." This internal recognition, this resonance occurring at the cellular or soul level, is a very strong indicator that the theme of pacts touches something personal and relevant in your own spiritual history. Trust these visceral reactions; they are the language of the soul pointing to areas worthy of investigation.

The process of identifying these signs is like assembling a complex puzzle about your own spiritual life. Each clue—a repetitive pattern, a symbolic dream, a habitual phrase, an intuitive reaction—is a piece. In the beginning, the pieces may seem disconnected, but as you patiently gather them with care and attention, a clearer picture may start to emerge. It is important not to jump to premature conclusions or get carried away by fantasy. Simply observe, collect the clues, and document your insights.

For this reason, it is highly recommended to keep a journal or notebook dedicated to this investigation. Write down the questions that resonated most with you and the responses or feelings that surfaced. Record relevant dreams, observed synchronicities, the phrases you find yourself repeating. Describe the physical or emotional sensations that arise when reflecting on these themes. This record will become a valuable map of your inner territory—a repository of data that will prove extremely useful as we advance to the next stages: exploring the spiritual memories that may hold the key to the origin of these pacts, and finally, undertaking the work of release.

This ongoing practice of self-observation is not only about uncovering a hidden origin or tracing the genealogy of an ancient pact; it is above all an act of presence with oneself—a gesture of loving listening to the soul. The journal thus becomes an extension of your field of consciousness—a place where intuition can take shape, where subtle insights become visible, and where small, previously unnoticed signs begin to form a coherent whole. As this inner map takes shape, spontaneous memories often start to emerge, accompanied by feelings of recognition. What once seemed like a mere hypothesis begins to gain texture and emotional depth. At this point, the investigation deepens, touching more sensitive layers that require care, patience, and, above all, internal honesty.

What is most transformative in this process is realizing that the signs do not arise to imprison but to liberate. They are not accusations from the past but invitations from the present. They point to areas where the energy of life remains trapped, calling for release. When we attentively listen to these calls—the recurring pattern, the persistent emotion, the repeating dream, the weighty phrase—we take the first step toward a reunion with forgotten parts of ourselves. It is as if the soul, through these symbolic and emotional codes, seeks our conscious collaboration to rewrite its story, to break bonds that no longer serve, and to restore the natural flow of existence.

The clarity born from this recognition prepares the ground for the work of release with much greater depth and effectiveness. The mind no longer resists, the heart opens, and the soul feels seen. When we know where to look, when we understand the signs as messages rather than sentences, we become capable of acting with consciousness and precision. Identifying the traces of spiritual pacts is, therefore, more than an analytical exercise—it is the beginning of healing. And with this beginning, the journey toward liberation ceases to be a spiritual abstraction and becomes a concrete reality, traveled step by step, with presence, courage, and truth.

Chapter 21
Spiritual Memory

The phase of personal investigation, which begins with the search for signs and evidence of ancient pacts in our lives, provides us with a preliminary map—a set of clues pointing to the possible existence of unresolved bonds. However, to truly understand the nature and power of these ties, we often need to go beyond the present symptoms and seek their origin—the moment and context in which they were forged. This invites us to dive into the deep waters of our own consciousness, to explore territories that transcend the ordinary biographical memory of this existence. We enter here the realm of spiritual memory, the vast library of the soul where the experiences, lessons, and, crucially, the commitments assumed throughout its long journey are archived.

Our capacity for recollection is not limited to the experiences lived since birth in this physical body. Beyond cerebral memory, accessible to daily consciousness, we possess much deeper records, engraved in the very essence of our spiritual being. This expanded memory encompasses not only the events of this life relegated to the subconscious, but also the recollections of other incarnations, the experiences lived in between lives, and the agreements and plans drawn up on higher levels of consciousness. It is within this soul archive that the roots of the most impactful pacts and vows often reside—those that continue to exert their hidden influence upon us. Accessing this spiritual memory, therefore, is not an exercise in morbid curiosity about the past, but a powerful tool for understanding the underlying causes of our present challenges and finding the keys to our liberation.

There are various paths and methods for accessing these deeper layers of memory. Some individuals feel drawn to more formal approaches, such as memory regression. Through deep relaxation techniques and guided visualization, often facilitated by a trained therapist, one may be led into an altered state of consciousness where scenes, feelings, or information from past lives can emerge. In these states, it is possible to relive or witness significant moments when oaths were made, vows assumed, or pacts sealed, gaining a direct understanding of the context and emotional charge involved. Another formal approach is the reading of the Akashic Records, where one seeks to access, through specific meditative practices or with the help of an intuitive reader, the "universal library" that contains the history of each soul, in order to obtain clear information about spiritual contracts and past commitments that may still be active and impacting the present life.

However, it is important to emphasize that one does not need to resort to formal methods or intermediaries to begin accessing one's own spiritual memory. For many people, profound insights may arise spontaneously through simpler and more accessible practices. Regular meditation, for example, by quieting the noise of the conscious mind and cultivating a state of inner receptivity, creates fertile ground for flashes of memory, symbolic images, or feelings related to past commitments to emerge naturally. Maintaining a clear intention during meditation—for instance, asking for understanding about the origin of a repetitive pattern or a specific blockage—can guide inner wisdom to bring forth relevant information. Likewise, sincere prayer, made with an open heart and a genuine desire for understanding, can open channels of communication with our higher self or spiritual guides, who may then provide insights through intuition, significant dreams, or synchronicities in the outer world.

Regardless of the chosen method, creating a conducive environment is essential to facilitate the emergence of these subtle memories. Seek moments of silence and tranquility where you will not be interrupted. Set a clear but gentle intention: the desire to know the truth about your spiritual past insofar as it serves your highest good in the present. Cultivate an open and receptive mind, willing to embrace whatever may arise—whether vivid images, bodily sensations, intense emotions, scattered words, or a sudden sense of "knowing" something without knowing how you know it. Avoid immediate judgment or the urge to rationally analyze everything that emerges; simply observe and record. Be patient and trust the process; the information may come in fragments over time, not necessarily in a single revealing session.

It is natural to feel some fear or apprehension at the prospect of accessing past life memories, especially those that may involve traumas or difficult commitments. Here, it is vital to trust the inherent wisdom of your own soul and the universe. Your deep consciousness will reveal only what you are truly ready to face, process, and integrate in the present moment. If knowing the origin of a specific pact is essential for your healing and evolution now, the information will find a safe and appropriate way to reach you. There will not be an avalanche of chaotic or unbearable memories. The process is usually gradual, guided by a loving intelligence that respects your limits and pace of growth.

Many people who have ventured to explore their spiritual memory report profoundly transformative experiences. Upon discovering the origin of a vow of poverty in a monastic life, they finally understood their chronic struggles with money. By recalling an oath of vengeance made during an ancient war, they recognized the root of their recurring anger. By accessing the memory of a promise of eternal love made to a soulmate in another era, they realized why they felt so incomplete or unable to fully engage in new relationships. These discoveries, although sometimes painful at first, brought immense relief, liberating clarity, and a new meaning to the challenges they faced. They understood that they were not flawed beings, but souls carrying complex stories that needed to be understood and healed.

Therefore, the invitation is to explore your inner world without fear. The keys to unlocking the mysteries of your own patterns, blocks, and limitations lie in the depths of your expanded consciousness. Accessing spiritual memory is not an act of escapism into the past, but a courageous and necessary step to retrieve vital information that can illuminate your present and liberate your future.

Amidst this journey of inner revelations, it becomes increasingly clear that spiritual memory not only provides answers but also calls for responsibility. As memories of vows, pacts, and distant experiences emerge, we are called to embrace these revelations with maturity, aware that knowing the past is only the first step. True transformation occurs when we integrate this knowledge into our current life, revising our patterns in the light of what has been unveiled and making decisions more aligned with who we truly are today. It is not about carrying ancestral guilt, but about recognizing that, at some point, we were co-authors of choices that now offer us the chance for growth and liberation.

In this process, forgiveness emerges as one of the most powerful tools. Forgiving oneself for past mistakes, releasing others from invisible bonds sustained by pain or misunderstood loyalty, and consciously and compassionately undoing the knots that still tie us to stories that have already ended—all of this contributes to the reconfiguration of one's personal energy field. Spiritual memory, when embraced with humility, does not reinforce past identities but dissolves them into the continuous flow of evolution. It allows us to look back just enough to understand, to give thanks, and to move forward with greater lightness and purpose.

Recognizing the value of these memories is also recognizing the power we hold in the present. Each fragment recovered, each sensation rediscovered, each intuition validated, are pieces that help compose the soul's mosaic in its process of unification. The journey into spiritual memory is, at its essence, a journey of reconnection—with truth, with love, with the wholeness that has always been there, simply waiting to be remembered.

Chapter 22
Inherited Bonds

The exploration of spiritual memory opens doors for us to understand the origins of many of our challenges and limitations, tracing them back to commitments made by our own soul at some point along its vast journey. However, the tapestry of existence is woven with threads that intertwine in complex ways, and our individual story is inextricably linked to the story of those who came before us. Beyond the pacts and vows we ourselves have created, there exists another category of energetic bonds that can deeply influence our lives: the spiritual bonds inherited from our ancestors, from our family lineage. The shadow of the past that follows us may, at times, not be cast solely by our own past actions, but also by promises, curses, or agreements made by our forebears.

The idea that the actions and commitments of one generation can reverberate through the next is not new, and echoes in cultural and spiritual traditions around the world. From an energetic and karmic perspective, this may occur in various ways. One of them is through familial karmic inheritance. Just as we inherit physical traits and genetic predispositions, we may also inherit certain energetic burdens or karmic patterns that have become part of the family's morphogenetic field. A strong pact or a curse pronounced against an ancestor, if unresolved or unneutralized, can leave an energetic residue that transmits through generations, manifesting as tendencies toward certain misfortunes, illnesses, or behavioral patterns among descendants. Another avenue of influence may be more direct, through the action of ancestral spirits who, still trapped by their own vows or the consequences of their pacts, may consciously or unconsciously influence the lives of their incarnated relatives—whether through attachment, a desire for control, or even a distorted attempt at protection.

Examples of these dynamics abound in folklore and family stories. How many families carry legends of a "curse" that fell upon the lineage due to a sinister pact made by a distant ancestor in exchange for wealth or power? Or tales of recurring misfortunes attributed to a broken promise made to a saint or a protective family deity? Beyond folklore, we can observe more concrete and verifiable patterns in certain lineages: families where poverty seems an inescapable fate despite each generation's efforts; clans where tragic love stories are repeatedly reenacted with uncanny regularity; lineages marked by specific diseases that defy purely genetic explanations. Although multiple causes may contribute to these patterns, the spiritualist perspective suggests that an ancient collective vow, a promise made by an influential patriarch or matriarch, or an unresolved family pact may be at work as one of the underlying factors, creating an energetic field that predisposes the repetition of that specific destiny.

Within this complex family web, the spiritualist view points to an interesting phenomenon: often, a specific family member—perhaps one with greater spiritual sensitivity, higher awareness, or simply a more "ancient" soul committed to healing—may unconsciously take on the burden of redeeming the lineage from these ancient contracts. This person may feel the effects of the inherited bond more intensely in their own life—the limitations, the patterns, the suffering. They become the focal point where the unresolved energy of the family system concentrates, not as punishment but as opportunity. It is as if the soul of the family, in its quest for balance and evolution, appoints one of its members to carry the torch of awareness and undertake the necessary work to break the chains binding the entire clan. This person may feel an inexplicable inner calling to investigate the family's past, to seek transgenerational healing therapies, or may simply feel a disproportionate weight that propels them to search for deeper answers.

This invites us to expand our investigation beyond our personal memory and dive into the history of our own family. Become a genealogist of the soul. Talk to older relatives, listen carefully to the stories told about your ancestors, even those that seem like legends or superstitions. What difficulties did they face? Were there patterns of behavior or destiny that repeated? Are there accounts of promises made in moments of despair, fervent devotions to saints or specific entities in exchange for protection or miracles? Are there family secrets kept under lock and key, traumatic events or difficult decisions that no one speaks of? Often, it is precisely in the silence, in what remains unspoken, that the most important clues about hidden pacts or vows still vibrating in the family's energetic field reside. Also observe objective patterns: recurring illnesses, tendencies toward addictions, chronic financial struggles, relationship patterns, inexplicable geographical limitations.

One of the most powerful mechanisms that perpetuate these inherited bonds is unconscious family loyalty. Driven by a deep love and a primal need for belonging to our clan, we may unknowingly repeat the difficult destinies of our parents, grandparents, or great-grandparents. If they suffered from scarcity, we may unconsciously block our own prosperity so as not to "betray" them or feel guilty for having more than they did. If they lived through unhappy relationships, we may repeat that pattern to remain loyal to their experience. This invisible loyalty may even lead us to energetically uphold the vows they made, living under the limitations of promises that were never ours, simply out of an unconscious desire to honor those who gave us life. It is a love that, though well-intentioned at its root, ends up perpetuating suffering across generations.

Recognizing that not all spiritual bonds affecting us were created directly by our individual soul greatly broadens our approach to liberation. The healing work is no longer limited to retrieving our own memories and resolving our personal pacts. It expands to include the possibility of identifying and releasing ties we have inherited from our lineage. This requires looking at our family history with compassion, without judgment, seeking to understand the difficult circumstances that may have led our ancestors to make certain commitments.

The beauty of this transgenerational work lies in its exponential healing potential. By identifying and consciously breaking an inherited pact that was limiting your own life, you are not only freeing yourself. On a subtle energetic level, you are also offering peace and resolution to your ancestors who may still be bound by that energy. Equally important, you are clearing the path for future generations of your family, ensuring that they no longer need to carry that specific burden. It becomes an act of loving service that reverberates through time, healing the past, liberating the present, and blessing the future of your entire family tree.

This awakening expands our role in the family story, inviting us to step forward not only as descendants but as active agents of healing. By recognizing the inherited bonds that run through us, we also come to realize the power we hold to transmute them. It is as if, by undertaking this inner work, we are answering a silent call issued by the generations who preceded us—a call to release the flow of life from ancient entanglements and allow new paths to open. This process, though often challenging, is profoundly transformative, for it dissolves not only the invisible ties that bound us to suffering, but also restores the dignity of forgotten stories, bringing light where there once was shadow.

As we consciously engage in this movement, we may turn to various healing tools such as family constellations, symbolic reconciliation rituals, release letters, or simple acts of respectful homage to our ancestors. Each act of listening and integration represents a step toward restoring the balance of the family system, allowing love to flow freely. It is not about seeking culprits in the past, but about looking with maturity at the choices made in other contexts, with the resources that were available at the time. When we touch these inherited wounds with compassion, we create the possibility of breaking automatic repetition and living with greater authenticity, assuming only what truly belongs to us.

By breaking the inherited spiritual bonds that have limited our full expression, we open space for a new relationship with our ancestry: one that is not based on silent loyalties and unconscious sacrifices, but on gratitude, freedom, and continuity. We begin to honor our ancestors not by repeating their pain, but by carrying forward their strength, wisdom, and history—now transmuted into lucid love. This is the true legacy we can leave: a lighter, more awakened family field, where those who come after us may walk their own path, free to write new chapters of their journey.

Chapter 23
Retrieving the Past

The journey of investigation has allowed us to gather valuable clues—repetitive patterns, symbolic dreams, intuitive reactions, family stories—that point to the possible presence of ancient pacts and vows influencing our lives. We may even have accessed fragments of spiritual memory that have offered glimpses into the origins of these commitments. Armed with this growing awareness, we now arrive at a crucial turning point: the moment not only to observe or understand but to actively engage with these memories and energies of the past, in an act of profound retrieval and inner healing. It is time to reach across time, not to relive the pain, but to liberate those parts of ourselves that remain trapped in the shackles of old promises.

This retrieval of the past is a delicate and sacred task, a loving reconnection with our own spiritual history. It requires courage to face moments that may have been painful, but above all, it demands immense compassion. Before beginning, find a moment and a place where you feel safe, calm, and undisturbed. Take a few deep breaths, centering yourself in the present moment. Set a clear intention for this inner work: the intention to understand, welcome, and lovingly release any pact or vow that no longer serves your highest good, asking for the support and guidance of your inner wisdom, your higher self, or your spiritual guides.

Allow yourself to enter a meditative, relaxed state. Visualize a timeline extending before and behind you, representing your soul's journey through this life and potentially others. With your focused intention, gently ask your inner wisdom to guide you to the moment and place where a specific pact—one you suspect to be active, perhaps identified through previous exercises—was originally made. Do not force the visualization; remain open to receiving the information in whatever form it comes—a clear image, a diffuse feeling, a stray word, a bodily sensation, or simply an inner knowing. Trust that you will be led to the point of origin relevant for your healing at this time.

As you find yourself "facing" this scene or feeling from the past, the most important attitude is one of radical compassion. Remember: you are observing a former version of yourself, a soul likely operating from a place of fear, pain, ignorance, despair, or perhaps naïve idealism. Resist any urge to judge, criticize, or condemn this past version for having made that vow. Instead, seek to understand the circumstances. Ask inwardly, with empathy: Why did this soul (myself, in another time) feel the need to make such a promise? What was the perceived threat? What pain was it trying to avoid? What need was it attempting to meet? Often, the pact was the only solution that consciousness could envision amid overwhelming circumstances or a limited understanding of life.

Welcome this past version of yourself as you would a beloved ancestor who has suffered. Mentally send them feelings of love, understanding, and acceptance. Acknowledge their struggle, their pain, their intention (even if the result of the pact has become limiting). This act of compassionate welcoming is already deeply healing and begins to soften the hardened energy of the old commitment.

Then begins the act of retrieval itself, which consists of three essential movements: recognition, honoring, and release. First, clearly recognize the pact made. You may say internally, addressing that past version: "I see you. I acknowledge the promise/vow/pact you made here, at this time, under these circumstances." Next, honor the intention or the lesson. Even the most limiting pacts may have originally carried a positive intention (to protect, survive, love, serve) or may have offered valuable lessons over time. Find something to honor: "I understand why you felt the need to do this. I honor your strength/your love/your intention to protect/your search for safety. I am grateful for the journey and the lessons this commitment, even though difficult, has brought us."

Finally, the culminating step: gently but firmly release that past self from the ongoing obligation of maintaining the pact. Affirm your present awareness, your broader perspective, and your current power of choice. Declare that circumstances have changed, that the lesson has been learned (or is being learned), and that the old agreement is no longer necessary or beneficial. You may use inner phrases, spoken with sincerity and love, such as: "You did the best you could at that time, with the awareness you had. The situation is different now. I, in the present, with greater resources and understanding, choose to release us both from this promise. In love and gratitude for the lesson, I declare this vow complete." Or perhaps: "I acknowledge your fear and your need at that time. I thank you for your attempt to guide or protect us through this vow. That time has passed. I now take responsibility for our safety and happiness in a new way. I release you from this burden. We are free now." Feel the truth of these words resonating within you.

Many who engage in this kind of inner work report an immediate sense of relief, as if a physical or energetic weight has been lifted from their shoulders. They may feel warmth, tingling, waves of liberating emotion (tears of relief rather than sadness), or a profound sense of peace and integration. It is as if, by lovingly retrieving and releasing that part of themselves trapped in the past, an ancestral energetic knot unravels, allowing vital energy to flow more freely once again.

This exercise of retrieving the past, though carried out on the symbolic and inner plane, is a psychomagical act of great power. It communicates to the subconscious, the energetic field, and perhaps even to the Akashic Records that a fundamental shift has taken place, that an old program has been deactivated at its source. It decisively prepares the inner ground, loosening the energetic roots of the pact and making the more practical steps of breaking and transformation, which we will explore next, much easier and more effective.

As this work of retrieval is repeated or deepened over time, something essential begins to occur: a new internal narrative forms—broader, more mature, less bound to the pain and rigidity of past promises. Instead of defining ourselves by inherited or assumed limitations, we begin to see ourselves as conscious co-authors of our own journey. This shift in perception is subtle but profound. We are no longer simply seeking to free ourselves from an isolated pact but to cultivate a new relationship with time, with our choices, and with our previous selves. We begin to see clearly that each retrieved fragment is also a piece of vital power returning to our field, strengthening our presence in the now.

This process also expands our empathy for others. By understanding the origins of our own vows and conditioning, we become less prone to judge the repetitions and patterns of others. We come to recognize that each person carries, in their silence, a profound story that may extend beyond this lifetime, and this invites listening, respect, and compassion. Thus, individual healing quietly transforms into a seed of collective healing. For as we release our own bonds, we also contribute to the weakening of collective energetic structures sustained for centuries by shared fears, pains, and illusions. A vow broken with love can dissolve resonances that had imprisoned many.

In this way, the past ceases to be a prison and becomes a sacred territory of reconciliation. Retrieval is no longer an attempt at repair, but a reunion—with one's soul in its wholeness, with cycles seeking completion, and with the freedom to live more presently and creatively. The personal timeline is no longer merely a succession of wounds, but a path filled with opportunities for healing and reinvention. By closing the doors that need to be closed, we open portals to new beginnings, anchored not in blind repetition, but in lucid choice.

Chapter 24
Spiritual Autonomy

The inner work of retrieving the past, of finding and compassionately welcoming those versions of ourselves who made ancient pacts and vows, reveals a fundamental and deeply liberating truth: the power to undo these bonds ultimately resides within ourselves. Before we delve into the practical techniques and rituals for breaking these ties, it is essential to firmly anchor in our consciousness the principle of spiritual autonomy. This is the understanding that each soul is sovereign over its own energetic field, its evolutionary choices, and the contracts it establishes, and that it possesses the innate authority and capacity to modify or end the commitments that no longer serve its growth.

The spiritual journey is intrinsically personal. No one, no matter how wise or powerful they may seem, can know the depths of our soul, the full story of our experiences, or the exact resonance of an oath made in bygone times as intimately as we do in our deepest levels. Even if conscious memory fails, cellular and soul wisdom retains the information. Therefore, no one is more qualified than the individual themselves to sense the truth about their commitments, to assess their current validity, and to make the sovereign decision to uphold, modify, or release them. Spiritual autonomy is the recognition of this inherent power and responsibility in every conscious being. It is claiming the right to be the author of one's own spiritual story, rather than a mere spectator or victim of external forces or unchangeable past decisions.

This understanding is particularly crucial in the context of releasing pacts, as it is a territory where vulnerability and fear can easily lead to the search for external solutions and the surrender of one's own power. It is important to clearly and calmly warn of the real danger of encountering unscrupulous individuals—so-called "gurus," "mediums," or "sorcerers"—who exploit others' desperation, promising to break curses, annul vows, or remove "attachments" in exchange for exorbitant sums of money or emotional dependency. These charlatans operate by feeding fear and the belief in personal powerlessness, positioning themselves as the sole holders of the necessary power for liberation. Surrendering our personal power and resources to such figures is not only ineffective in most cases but can also create new energetic and psychological entanglements that are even harder to unravel.

This does not mean, by any means, that we cannot seek or receive help in our process. There are, indeed, serious therapists, ethical spiritual counselors, competent energy healers, and loving guides who can offer valuable support. They can help us access memories, understand hidden dynamics, process difficult emotions, strengthen our energy, or teach us self-liberation techniques. They may act as facilitators, as mirrors, as sources of inspiration and encouragement. However, their role is always to assist, to support, to empower the individual to do their own inner work. True liberation, the kind that is deep and lasting, always occurs from the inside out, driven by the conscious and sovereign decision of the soul itself. A genuine guide will always respect and strengthen your autonomy, never fostering dependence or positioning themselves as the sole source of power. Discernment is key: help that empowers and teaches us to stand on our own is welcome; that which fosters dependence and diminishes us must be avoided.

The foundation of this autonomy lies in trust in our own divine potential. Every human being, regardless of their history or present circumstances, carries within them a spark of the universe's creative force—a direct connection to the source of all power and love. This inner divine essence possesses the inherent capacity to dissolve any self-created limitation, including the energetic bonds of ancient pacts and vows. When we align our intention with this profound truth, when we believe in our capacity for healing and transformation, and when we act from a place of self-love and sincere desire for evolution, we mobilize an immense power capable of dissolving any bondage. We do not need intermediaries to access this force; it is our spiritual birthright.

It is important to balance this assertion of autonomy with the comforting truth that we are not alone on this journey. As we claim our inner power, we also open ourselves to receive the support of higher dimensions—our own inner wisdom, our spiritual guides, angels, ascended masters, and the loving intelligence of the universe, according to our personal beliefs. This support is always available, ready to assist us when we sincerely ask and are open to receive. However, even with all this assistance, it is we who steer the helm of our vessel. The decision to change course, to cut the ropes of old anchors, to sail toward freedom, is ours alone and non-transferable. Spiritual support gives us strength, clarity, and protection, but it does not absolve us of responsibility for our choices and actions.

Cultivating this deep sense of spiritual autonomy and self-trust is, therefore, the essential preparation for the practical steps of dissolving pacts that will follow. Without this inner conviction, rituals and techniques may become hollow gestures, lacking the soul force necessary to bring about real change on the energetic level. Faith in our own capacity to free ourselves, combined with pure intention and the spiritual support we invoke, is the true engine of transformation. By the end of this chapter, it is our hope that the reader feels not only informed about the importance of autonomy but truly empowered, secure, and ready to move forward. You have the power, you have the authority, you have the necessary support.

This full recognition of spiritual autonomy repositions us before every challenge as conscious co-creators of our own reality. It is not about denying the complexity of the bonds or invisible influences, but about remembering that, no matter how intricate the web of energies in which we are entangled, there is always a way out—and that way begins with our internal decision. When we stop waiting for an external savior and instead assume the role of protagonists in our journey, something powerful happens: the field around us begins to respond differently. We begin to radiate a frequency of sovereignty, of clarity, which in itself repels that which resonates with fear, submission, and helplessness.

This shift does not happen abruptly or artificially. It is the soul's maturation, a gradual return to its own center. And this return can be sustained by simple yet consistent practices: the habit of listening to one's own intuition before following any external guidance, the exercise of asking oneself, "Does this make sense to me?" or "Does this strengthen my freedom or further imprison me?" and, above all, the cultivation of a constant presence in the now, which is where our true power manifests. In doing so, we recognize that no past pact, no matter how ancient or dense it may seem, can be stronger than the free and conscious decision of an awakened soul in the present.

Therefore, claiming spiritual autonomy is not merely a necessary step toward breaking pacts—it is a stance toward life itself. It is choosing to live from the inside out, with one's feet firmly rooted in one's own truth, open to the help that liberates, yet impervious to the illusions that enslave. As we anchor this awareness, the path of liberation unfolds with greater fluidity and integrity. The next step, then, will not be taken from a place of doubt or lack, but from a strengthened center that knows the power to change lies right here: in the awakened, free, and sovereign heart of every being.

Chapter 25
Free Decision

Strengthened by the understanding of our spiritual autonomy and the recognition of our inherent power to shape our energetic destiny, we now stand at the threshold of transformative action. After the journey of investigation, recognition, and inner retrieval, before us rises the first effective step—the primal gesture that truly initiates the process of releasing the pacts and vows that bind us: the free and conscious decision to break these ties. This is not a step to be taken lightly, but rather an act of profound personal sovereignty, a moment in which the soul, armed with clarity and intention, affirms its will to move forward, free from the chains of the past.

Everything we have explored so far—the nature of pacts, their consequences, the identification of their signs, the access to spiritual memory, the understanding of autonomy—converges at this focal point. The awareness we have gained now allows us to make a choice that may not have been possible at the moment when the original commitment was made, often in the midst of despair, ignorance, or pressure. Now, with a broader understanding and a stronger connection to our inner power, we can deliberately choose a new direction. The invitation is for you, the reader, to affirm with the full clarity of your will, with the calm strength of your awakened soul, that you now choose to release yourself from that ancient commitment which no longer serves your growth and well-being.

Within the great framework of the spiritual laws that govern existence, free will holds a place of prominence. It is the sacred prerogative of the conscious soul to choose its path, to learn its lessons, to create its reality. In the face of a firm, clear, and conscious decision by the soul to free itself from a self-imposed bond, no pact, no matter how ancient or solemn, can remain irrevocable. Energy responds to focused intention and sovereign will. When you declare, from the depths of your being, your decision to cancel an old vow, you are exercising your divine right to redirect your own energy and rewrite your spiritual contracts.

This moment of internal decision is almost like a magical "click," an instant when the energetic configuration begins to shift fundamentally. It is the turning point. By saying to yourself with unshakable conviction: "I now decide, in my full right and power, to cancel and undo any pact, vow, or oath [specify, if known, or use general terms] that binds and limits me. I choose freedom," you initiate the process of unbinding the subtle chains. The clarity of your intention sends a direct command to your subconscious to begin deactivating old programs. Your statement reverberates throughout your energetic field, starting to dissolve the invisible ties. You signal to the universe your new choice, aligning yourself with the energies of liberation and autonomy. The conscious decision is the first and most crucial act of breaking the bond.

Reflect on the entire journey that has brought you to this point. You have understood the nature of pacts, investigated their possible effects on your life, perhaps glimpsed their origins, and recognized your own spiritual authority. Realize, in this moment, that you are no longer a hostage of the past. The awareness you have acquired is power. The knowledge of hidden dynamics grants you the ability to intervene in them. You are no longer operating blindly, reacting to invisible forces. You now have clarity and, therefore, power over the situation. The shadow of the past may still exist, but you now hold the lantern of awareness, ready to illuminate and transform it. The decision to free yourself is the ultimate expression of this reclaimed power.

To anchor this internal decision and endow it with even greater strength, it may be helpful to perform a small mental or written ritual that symbolizes your commitment to yourself. Find a moment of stillness. You may simply close your eyes, place your hand over your heart, and declare your decision aloud or silently, feeling the truth of your words resonating in every cell of your body. Or, if you prefer a more concrete gesture, take a sheet of paper and write your declaration of freedom. It may be something simple, such as: "I, [your name], on this date, declare my irrevocable decision to renounce and release all pacts, vows, and oaths, known or unknown, from this life or past lives, that no longer serve my highest good and spiritual evolution. I choose freedom, joy, and wholeness. Signed, [your name and date]." Keep this paper in a meaningful place or use it in a later ritual (as we will explore ahead), but the act of writing and signing already marks a formal and powerful commitment to yourself.

It is essential that this decision be imbued with a quality of loving determination. This is not an act of anger toward the past or violent rejection of the part of yourself that made the pact. On the contrary, it is an act of deep self-love, a recognition that you deserve to live free from self-imposed limitations. It is also an act of compassion for your past self, releasing it from a burden it no longer needs to carry. The firmness of the decision must come from clarity and love, not denial or aggression. A serene and loving determination holds far greater transformative power than rebellion.

Celebrate this moment. The awakening of conscious free will in relation to these ancient bonds is a fundamental milestone on the spiritual journey. The sincere decision, born of understanding and autonomy, is the master key that begins to turn in the lock of the invisible prison. The door may not yet be fully open, but the mechanism has been activated. From this point forward, all subsequent steps—the techniques of cutting ties, the rituals of release, the work of forgiveness—will serve to consolidate and manifest the freedom you have just chosen.

This moment of choosing, with clarity and serenity, to break with pacts that no longer serve, marks not only an energetic shift but the birth of a new state of being. In deciding, you are planting a seed that will blossom into freedom, new life patterns, and more authentic relationships with yourself and the world. The free decision is more than a symbolic gesture—it is a realignment of the soul with its current truth, a conscious redirection of its spiritual trajectory. Even if the effects of this choice do not immediately manifest in every aspect of life, something fundamental has already shifted on the subtle plane: you no longer walk the same path as before.

This choice may also ripple beyond your own individual field. Often, when we make a decision so deeply aligned with our highest good, we energetically influence the environment around us. We change how we position ourselves in life, which by itself may dissolve resistance, inspire others to reflect on themselves, and transform family patterns that once seemed unchangeable. The free decision is not merely an ending of what no longer serves, but the beginning of a phase of life more aligned with our present purpose, with greater lightness, awareness, and authenticity. It is the portal to a new stage of the journey, where we no longer act in reaction to the past but in conscious creation of the future.

Therefore, honor this moment for the milestone it is. Hold this choice within you as a luminous anchor for the days when doubts may arise. Return to it whenever necessary, reaffirming your commitment to your freedom and the expansion of your awareness. The free decision is the fertile ground upon which the next steps will be built, with more confidence, clarity, and personal power. It is the beginning of a passage toward a life lived with truth, presence, and spiritual autonomy—a life that honors not only who you have been but, above all, who you now choose to become.

Chapter 26
Breaking Ties

The free and conscious decision to liberate ourselves from old pacts and vows is the key that turns the ignition, the act of will that signals to the universe and to our own soul the intention to change course. However, for this decision to translate into effective and lasting liberation, an additional step is often necessary: the direct energetic work of breaking the subtle bonds that have kept us tied to these commitments. Having clearly stated our intention and claimed our spiritual autonomy, we now enter the domain of energetic action—a practical process of cutting or dissolving the invisible connections that have sustained old patterns.

This work of breaking ties is most effective when carried out from an elevated and centered state of consciousness. Before beginning, prepare your space and your energy. Find a quiet moment where you will not be interrupted. Sit or lie down comfortably. Breathe deeply and calmly several times, releasing bodily tension and mental concerns with each exhale. Connect with your inner center, with your divine spark. You may say a prayer aligned with your faith, asking for protection, clarity, and the assistance of the forces of light that accompany you. Or you may simply visualize a radiant light—perhaps golden, white, or violet—surrounding your entire being, creating a sacred and safe space for the work ahead. The goal is to raise your vibration, dispel dissonant energies, and align with your highest spiritual power.

In this heightened state of connection and clarity, invite your inner awareness to turn toward the pacts or vows from which you have chosen to free yourself. You need not have an exhaustive list or recall every detail. You may focus on a specific vow you have identified, or work with the general intention of releasing all obsolete commitments. Allow your intuition to reveal to you—or simply sense or "know"—how these bonds manifest in your energy field. You may perceive them as cords, threads, webs, or even chains extending from certain parts of your body (heart, mind, solar plexus, back) or from your aura, connecting you to people, places, ideas, or energies from the past. Do not worry if the visualization is not perfectly clear; intention and feeling matter more than visual clarity. Trust your ability to perceive what needs to be released.

Now, with your imagination active and your intention firmly focused on your decision for freedom, proceed with the visualization of breaking these ties. Choose the image or technique that resonates most with you, the one you feel is most powerful and effective in your heart:

The Sword of Light: Visualize yourself wielding a brilliant sword of pure light (or ask a being of light, such as Archangel Michael, to wield it). With decisive and precise movements, see or feel this sword cutting through each cord, each chain binding you to the pact. Perceive the ties snapping and your energy being released.

The Violet Flame: Mentally invoke the powerful Violet Flame of spiritual transmutation. Visualize this sacred flame enveloping the energetic ties, lovingly consuming them, dissolving not only the connection but also transmuting any negative or residual energy associated with the pact into pure light. See the ties disintegrating into luminous particles.

Angelic Assistance: Request help from your guardian angels, spiritual guides, or other beings of light in whom you trust. Visualize them surrounding you, working with love and delicacy to untie the knots, unravel the threads, or dissolve the chains with their hands of light, gently freeing you from the bonds.

Other Images: You may use other images that feel appropriate to you—perhaps visualizing scissors of light cutting the threads, pure water washing away the connections, or a specific vibrational sound breaking the bonds.

What matters in any chosen technique is to engage your intention and feeling. Truly feel the breaking happening. Feel the disconnection. Feel the once-bound energy being released. It is not enough to simply "think" of the cutting; you must "feel" the liberation occurring on the energetic level.

To enhance this visualization work, use words of power. Clear and confident affirmations, spoken aloud or mentally, anchor your intention and command the energy. Try phrases such as:

"I now break, in the name of my divine essence and my sovereign free will, all pacts, vows, and oaths, known and unknown, that limit me and prevent me from living my full expression. I am free, whole, and complete now!"

"By the power of the Light that I Am, I dissolve and undo at this very moment all energetic ties that bind me to [mention the subject of the vow, if known]. All energy returns to its origin, purified and transmuted into love. I reclaim my energy and my sovereignty. I am free!"

"With love and gratitude for the lessons learned, I now release my past and all commitments that no longer serve my present. I cut all ties. I am free to create my life from this moment forward."

Speak these affirmations with authority, feeling their truth resonate within your being. It is important to perform this process with conviction in your power to free yourself, but also with respect—respect for your soul's journey, respect for your past self who made the pact, and respect for any other energies or consciousnesses that may have been involved (even as the intention is to disconnect from them). Liberation is an act of sovereignty, not of aggression.

Be aware that some vows or pacts—especially very old ones, those heavily charged with emotion, or those involving multiple parties—may require more than one tie-breaking session. Trust your intuition. If you feel the work is not yet complete, or if you perceive certain patterns or feelings persist, do not hesitate to repeat the process at another time, perhaps focusing more specifically on a bond you still sense present. Loving perseverance is an important key.

At the end of each tie-breaking session, take a moment to breathe and feel the effects. Many people report an immediate sense of lightness, as if a weight has been lifted. There may be renewed mental clarity, a sense of expansion in the chest, a more vibrant flow of energy throughout the body, or simply a deep sense of peace and relief. Welcome these sensations as confirmation that the subtle ties have been broken and that energy has begun to flow more freely.

This practical phase of energetic release represents more than the dissolution of invisible connections; it is the tangible expression of a profound choice. Each image visualized, each word spoken with clear intention, is a symbolic gesture that reverberates in the subtle fabric of our spiritual field. This gesture, carried out consciously, becomes real action. Energy obeys the vibration of will, and when that will is guided by clarity, respect, and self-love, transformation becomes inevitable. The soul recognizes this movement as an act of returning to itself, a reunion with its original integrity, free from the layers accumulated through vows that no longer resonate with its present essence.

At the same time, this work creates inner space for the new. With the release of old ties, our energy field reorganizes, freeing areas that had been occupied by repetitive patterns or dissonant connections. This reorganization may manifest as subtle changes in thoughts, in the body, in emotions—or even in our relationships and external circumstances. It is common that, after breaking a deep pact, new opportunities arise, decisions become clearer, and relationships naturally redefine themselves. This happens because, by releasing energy previously committed to the past, we regain our ability to act with greater freedom in the present, making choices that truly reflect who we are now.

Therefore, allow yourself to embrace the moment after the ritual as a space for integration. Be silent, give thanks, trust. This silence is not emptiness: it is the fertile field where new possibilities will begin to sprout. And remember that breaking ties is not an abrupt rupture with the soul's history, but a loving reconciliation with it. It is a turning point where we cease to be defined by pacts of pain and begin to be guided by a conscious commitment to freedom, presence, and inner truth. It is the subtle dance between intention and action, between healing and creation—and it is in this space that the soul, at last, fully breathes.

Chapter 27
Symbolic Ritual

The inner work of choosing freedom and the energetic act of breaking subtle ties are fundamental and powerful steps in the journey of releasing old pacts. They operate in the invisible dimensions of intention and energy, undoing the bonds at their most fundamental level. However, our human experience also unfolds on the physical plane, and our psyche—especially its deeper, unconscious layers—responds strongly to concrete gestures, to ceremonial acts that anchor internal changes in tangible reality. Therefore, to consolidate the breaking of pacts and fully integrate the new reality of freedom, performing a personal symbolic ritual can be an immensely valuable complementary step.

The power of ritual lies in its ability to speak a language that the intellect often cannot reach: the language of symbols, metaphors, and meaningful actions. While conscious decision-making operates in the rational mind and the breaking of ties works in the energetic field, the symbolic ritual communicates the transformation to our whole being—body, emotions, unconscious, and spirit. Physical gestures performed with clear intention act as bridges, helping both mind and heart to assimilate the depth of the internal change that has occurred. A well-performed ritual marks a transition, creates a visible marker between the "before" and the "after," and helps seal the new reality in our consciousness.

It is essential to understand that there is no single or correct formula for performing such a ritual. Its effectiveness does not lie in the complexity of its props or adherence to external dogmas, but in the sincerity of the intention, the faith invested in the act, and the personal resonance it holds for you. The invitation is for you to create a small ceremony that makes sense within your own worldview and spiritual connection. It may be extremely simple: lighting a candle with a specific intention, washing your hands in running water while visualizing the cleansing of old bonds, ringing a bell to mark the end of one cycle and the beginning of another, burying an object that represents the pact, or burning a piece of paper on which your intentions have been written. What matters is that the chosen act clearly represents to you the idea of purification, release from the past, and a new beginning in freedom.

To illustrate the possibilities, let us consider a detailed example. You might take a piece of paper and write a letter, perhaps addressed to your past self, to the universe, or to the energies involved in the pact. In this letter, describe the pacts or vows from which you wish to free yourself (whether specific or general), mention how they have affected you, and reaffirm your sovereign decision to end them now. Express gratitude for the lessons learned, even the difficult ones. Then, take this letter to a safe place—perhaps outdoors, at a fireplace, in a metal sink, or in an appropriate cauldron. With care and respect, set the paper on fire. As you watch the flames consume the letter, keep your intention focused on release and transformation. You may pray, chant a mantra, or simply state aloud or mentally: *"With this flame, I transform these old vows into ashes. I release their energy from my life. May the ashes return to the earth, and may my life be renewed in the light of freedom. So it is."* Watch the smoke rise, visualizing all the past energy dissipating. Afterwards, collect the ashes (once cooled) and scatter them in nature (earth, running water), or dispose of them respectfully, symbolizing the definitive end of that cycle.

Another example might involve the use of a candle. Choose a candle that represents purification and new beginnings (traditionally white) or transmutation (violet). Create a small altar or sacred space, perhaps with flowers, crystals, or images that inspire you. Light the candle with the clear intention that its flame symbolizes your awakened consciousness and your power to dissolve unwanted ties. Gaze at the flame for a few moments, breathing deeply. Then declare with conviction that this sacred light is now consuming all ties, pacts, vows, and oaths that limit you. Affirm your freedom, your wholeness, your new choice of life. You may remain in meditation before the candle, visualizing the ties dissolving into the light, until you feel the process is complete. Allow the candle to burn for some time (or completely, if it is safe to do so), as a silent witness to your liberation.

The physical object used in the ritual—the paper that turns to ashes, the candle that burns into light, the water that carries away what you release—acts as a tangible symbol of your intention and of the transformation taking place. Our ancestral psyche understands this language. By witnessing with our own senses the transformation or disappearance of the symbol, a deep part of us registers that something has truly ended, that a concrete change has occurred. The ritual helps "officialize" the breaking of ties, inscribing it not only at the energetic level but also in psychological and emotional memory.

Always remember: the power does not lie in the object itself, but in the intention, the sincerity, and the faith you invest in the act. Trust your intuition to create the ritual that is most meaningful and powerful for you at this moment in your journey. Whether simple or elaborate, what matters is that it clearly and meaningfully marks this fundamental transition.

Symbolic rituals not only express an internal decision but also serve as a direct language between the conscious and unconscious, between the visible and the invisible. When one consecrates a space, a time, and an action to symbolize the break with the old, one allows the soul to align with the new configuration of freedom. The human psyche is deeply sensitive to these symbolic markers, and even if the rational mind doubts, there is an inner layer that understands, accepts, and reorganizes itself around the new reality. This becomes even more powerful with recurrence—by revisiting the symbolic act with personal variations over time, the integration process deepens, consolidating the new state as something not only desired but lived and fully integrated.

Furthermore, the ritual can serve as a channel for reconnecting with aspects of spirituality often forgotten in daily life. By allowing ourselves a conscious pause to create a symbolic gesture, we reclaim the sacredness of existence. This does not mean adopting dogmas or following external traditions, but rather discovering one's own spiritual language, the unique way each individual accesses the mystery and the sacred. In creating a ritual imbued with freedom and personal meaning, one opens space for a living spirituality that pulses in harmony with the cycles of the inner life. This reconnection with the personal sacred transforms the ritual into more than a closing act: it also becomes a seed of spiritual renewal.

And it is at this intersection between gesture and intention, between symbol and feeling, that something profound is reconfigured. The breaking of pacts ceases to be merely an energetic or mental decision—it begins to inhabit the body, the memory, the soul. In performing your symbolic ritual, you are not only releasing the past: you are fully embracing the role of conscious creator of your own journey. This is the true meaning of attained freedom—not the absence of bonds, but the sovereign presence of your own will illuminated by inner truth.

Chapter 28
Forgiveness and Release

The sovereign decision has been made, the energetic ties have been consciously severed, and a symbolic ritual may have sealed, on the physical plane, the intention to leave behind old pacts and vows. We feel a new lightness, an open space. However, the journey toward complete freedom rarely ends there. Often, even after these crucial steps, emotional residues tied to the history of those commitments may remain in the heart—unresolved grievances, lingering guilt, resentments toward others or toward ourselves. These lingering emotions act as subtle anchors, preventing us from fully navigating the clear waters of the present. Therefore, an essential step to consolidate our liberation is the deep and sincere work of forgiveness and emotional release.

Pacts and vows, especially those made during times of great intensity or that had difficult consequences, are often intertwined with a complex web of feelings. There may be anger toward the person who induced us to make a harmful oath, or toward the entity with whom we feel bound in an unfavorable agreement. There may be deep resentment toward the circumstances that drove us to an act of desperation. Guilt may linger for having made a vow that limited our life or that of others, or for having failed to fulfill an important promise. There may even be residual sorrow directed at God or fate for allowing us to go through such trials. As long as these emotional burdens remain unacknowledged, unprocessed, and unreleased, they will continue to keep us energetically connected, in some way, to the vibration of that past.

The invitation now is to undertake an honest and courageous inner inventory. Set aside time to feel, in your heart, what emotions are still alive regarding the pacts you are working to release. Allow yourself to recognize, without judgment, whether there is still anger, grief, resentment, guilt, fear, or sadness associated with them. Identify, if possible, to whom or to what these feelings are directed. Writing about it may help bring clarity. This is not about wallowing in negativity, but about mapping the emotional knots that still need to be untied so that liberation may be truly complete.

Once these points of emotional pain are identified, the path to dissolution leads through the portal of forgiveness. It is crucial to understand forgiveness not in its popular sense of "forgive and forget" or of necessarily reconciling with those who harmed us, but in its deeper spiritual sense: the act of freeing oneself from the weight of negative emotions that imprison us. In this context, forgiveness is an act of spiritual intelligence and self-love. It is the recognition that carrying resentment, guilt, or hatred is like taking poison and expecting the other to die. The energy of these dense emotions harms us primarily, keeping us chained to the past and blocking the flow of love and joy in our present life. To forgive is to release the emotional chains that bind us to pain—not to benefit the other, but to free ourselves.

To assist in this process, you may perform a forgiveness exercise. Once again, find your calm and centered space. Bring to mind the person or people involved in the situation of the pact (including your own past self). If you feel comfortable, visualize them before you, bathed in a gentle light. Allow yourself to express, mentally or softly aloud, any pain or sorrow you still feel—not as accusation, but as an honest sharing of your experience. Then take a deep breath and make the conscious decision to forgive. Say sincerely, from your heart: *"I choose to forgive you [name of the person or 'my past self'] for your role in this situation. I now release all anger, all resentment, all judgment I have held toward you. I release you, and I release myself."* Feel the heavy energy dissipating. If appropriate, also ask for forgiveness for your part—for any harm or pain you may have caused, consciously or unconsciously. And, most importantly, direct forgiveness toward yourself: *"I completely forgive myself for having made this pact/vow, for having broken it (if applicable), for any suffering it may have caused me or others. I did the best I could with the awareness I had at that time. I fully accept and love myself unconditionally."* Conclude by declaring mutual release: *"I release you, I release myself. May we all move forward in peace, free from this bond."* Visualize the emotional cords dissolving into light.

It is important to extend this forgiveness to the broader spiritual level as well. If you have harbored resentment toward God, destiny, life, or any entity for the difficulties related to the pact, this is the moment to seek reconciliation. Strive to transmute the sorrow into understanding, recognizing that even the most arduous experiences have brought valuable lessons to your soul. Release any feelings of having been wronged or punished. Affirm your trust in the greater wisdom of the universe and in your own ability to overcome and grow.

To seal this work of forgiveness and emotional release, a healing visualization can be very powerful. Focus on the area of your heart. With each inhalation, imagine you are breathing in a golden light—warm, bright, and radiant—the pure energy of divine love, compassion, and unconditional forgiveness. Feel this light filling your chest, softening any hardness, warming any coldness. With each exhale, visualize releasing a gray or dark smoke—representing all accumulated sorrow, guilt, fear, and resentment. Continue breathing this way: inhaling golden light, exhaling dense energy, until you feel your heart fully filled with light, with every dark corner illuminated, the space where there was once pain now vibrating with peace, love, and acceptance. Feel this light expanding throughout your entire being.

The final message of this chapter is clear and transformative: only through complete forgiveness—of oneself and of all involved—does the release from old pacts become total and definitive. Forgiveness is the universal solvent that dissolves the last energetic and emotional remnants that could keep us tied to the past. When no guilt remains to imprison us and no resentment binds us to the old story, the pact loses all power over us. The energy that once sustained it has been withdrawn and transmuted into love and wisdom. The heart, finally free from the weight of unresolved emotions, can then open fully to joy, trust, and the infinite possibilities of the present.

The process of deep forgiveness is, in essence, a return to the soul's center, where there are no more accusations or defenses, only the serene presence of what is. By releasing the past with honesty and compassion, we are not denying the pain that was experienced, but positioning ourselves above it, in a place of inner sovereignty. This movement restores to us the power to choose, to create, and to love without the distorted filters of resentment. Anger transforms into discernment, guilt into responsibility, and fear into wisdom. In this emotional alchemy, forgiveness becomes not just an isolated act, but an ongoing practice of liberation and self-love.

As this healing work advances, one realizes that forgiveness is not a favor granted to the other, nor a naïve concession—it is a profound gesture of self-care. In choosing to forgive, we give ourselves the chance to breathe freely, to live without the burden of what can no longer be changed. We release time trapped in memory and reclaim our presence in the now. Forgiveness, in this context, is like a river cleansing the banks of the past, fertilizing the present with previously unimagined possibilities. It connects us with a broader dimension of existence, where pain no longer needs to narrate our story.

And when the heart, purified, once again recognizes its fullness, a new silence emerges—not the silence of absence, but of filled presence. The journey of breaking old pacts finds here its true conclusion: not in the act of cutting, but in understanding, embracing, and moving forward in peace. The past ceases to be a prison and becomes a silent teacher. And life, now light, begins again with gentler eyes, steadier steps, and a soul truly free.

Chapter 29
Spiritual Protection

The path traveled thus far has been one of deep introspection, courage, and transformation. Through free choice, the energetic severing of ties, the symbolic ritual, and the healing balm of forgiveness, we have dismantled the invisible structures of pacts and vows that limited our expression and dimmed our light. We emerge from this process lighter, more aware, more whole. Yet the journey does not end with the demolition of the prison's old walls; it continues with the conscious task of inhabiting and protecting the newly acquired space of freedom. Just as a cleared field requires care to prevent the return of weeds, our renewed life benefits from establishing a consistent practice of spiritual protection.

After breaking free from old and deeply rooted energetic patterns, it is natural to experience a period of adjustment—perhaps even a temporary sense of vulnerability. Think of someone who has lived for a long time in a dark room and suddenly steps into the sunlight; the eyes need time to adapt, the skin feels the exposure in a new way. Likewise, as we free ourselves from the limiting "structures" of pacts, our energy field may feel more open, more exposed, before fully stabilizing in its new configuration of freedom. It is like leaving a prison: the open space is liberating, but may initially feel vast and unprotected. For this reason, it becomes important to actively strengthen our aura and clearly define our energetic space, ensuring that our freedom is sustained and that we are not easily susceptible to undesirable influences or relapses into old patterns.

There are simple and effective techniques that we can incorporate into our daily lives to nourish and protect our energy field. One of the most powerful is the conscious visualization of protective light. Set aside a few moments—perhaps in the morning upon waking or at night before sleep, or whenever you feel the need. Breathe deeply, center yourself, and visualize a bright and vibrant light—perhaps golden like the sun, white like divine purity, or violet like the flame of transmutation—forming a sphere, shield, or circle around your entire physical and etheric body. Feel this light as an impenetrable barrier against any negative energy, yet permeable to all love and goodness. See it sealing any cracks in your aura, strengthening your energetic boundaries. Hold this visualization for a few moments, feeling safe, protected, and radiant within this bubble of light. Practicing this regularly reinforces your energy field and creates a habit of protective self-care.

Prayer and the invocation of spiritual support are also valuable tools. Regardless of your faith tradition, addressing the Divine Source, God, the Universe, or your Higher Self with a sincere request for ongoing protection is a powerful act. You may simply say: *"I ask that divine light surround and protect me today, guiding my steps and keeping my energy field clear and safe."* You may also specifically call upon your spiritual guides, guardian angels, or benevolent mentors, asking them to guard your space, ward off negative influences, and help you maintain your vibration at a high level. Knowing that we are not alone and that we can rely on the assistance of the forces of light brings comfort and strengthens our sense of safety.

The mind is a fundamental instrument in maintaining our energetic protection. Our thoughts generate vibrations, and elevated, positive thoughts create a field of resonance that naturally repels denser energies. Cultivating the habit of using daily positive affirmations can be very effective. Create short, powerful phrases that reinforce your new reality of freedom and security, such as: *"I am divinely protected and guided at all times," "My energy field is strong, vibrant, and impervious to any negativity," "I walk in the light of my truth, free and sovereign," "I am grateful for my freedom and I maintain it with love and awareness."* Repeat these affirmations with conviction throughout the day, especially when you feel any doubt or vulnerability. This helps keep your mind attuned to goodness and strengthens your positive energetic signature.

Spiritual protection also involves conscious self-care on more practical levels. Pay attention to the quality of your own thoughts and emotions. Avoid feeding fears, resentments, or judgments, as these energies can weaken your protective field. Also, be mindful of the environments you frequent and the company you keep. Especially while your newfound freedom is still consolidating, it may be wise to avoid people or places strongly associated with old negative patterns or that leave you feeling drained or uncomfortable. Seek environments and companions that uplift you, nourish your soul, and respect your space. Continuing practices such as meditation, yoga, or spending time in nature also helps maintain balance and energetic strength.

For those who feel aligned, certain elements of nature can serve as additional aids in the work of energetic cleansing and protection. Crystals such as Black Tourmaline, Onyx, or Obsidian are traditionally known for their ability to absorb or repel negative energies. Clear Quartz and Selenite can help purify and elevate vibration. Incense such as White Sage, Palo Santo, or Frankincense can be used to smudge the body or environment, clearing stagnant energies. Baths with herbs like Rue, Guiné, Rosemary, Basil, or even coarse salt, can help discharge accumulated dense energies and revitalize the aura. However, it is important to remember that these elements are merely supports; the true source of protection resides within our inner state.

And this is the crucial point: the greatest protection does not come from amulets or external rituals, but from the vigilant and confident inner attitude of one who has truly taken the reins of their spiritual life. It is clarity of purpose, integrity of thought and action, will aligned with the greater good, unwavering faith in one's connection to divine light, and constant self-observation that build the most impenetrable shield. When we cultivate this inner strength, this conscious sovereignty, we become less susceptible to negative external influences. With firm will and spiritual light shining from within and radiating outward, we ensure that the old energetic ties of pacts find no anchoring points to return and that new limiting bonds do not easily form.

This active awareness of one's own vibration and energy field inaugurates a new stage in the journey: no longer focused solely on healing the past, but on the attentive cultivation of a present life that is strengthened, lucid, and aligned with the freedom attained. Spiritual protection should not be seen as a constant effort of isolation or defense, but as an act of care for oneself. It is a way of affirming daily: *"I value myself enough to care for my energy, to protect the light I now recognize within me."* In this sense, the practice of spiritual protection is also a continuous exercise of presence and self-respect.

As this new posture of loving protection is integrated, we begin to relate differently to the world. Spiritual sensitivity sharpens, allowing us to more clearly perceive what nourishes us and what drains us, what strengthens our soul and what threatens to disconnect us from our truth. It becomes easier to say no to what no longer resonates and yes to what promotes our expansion. Discernment is refined, and with it comes a gentle tranquility, born of knowing that we are caring for what is most precious: our very essence. Over time, this clarity transforms into confidence, and this confidence into lasting peace—not a naïve peace, but one born of continuous presence, conscious alignment, and loyalty to oneself.

And thus, the new space of freedom is consolidated: not as a momentary achievement, but as a continuous state of being, nourished daily by aligned choices and an authentic commitment to one's own light. Spiritual protection, when done with love and awareness, does not close us off from the world—on the contrary, it opens us to it with greater truth and wholeness, for we no longer fear losing what has already taken root as an essential part of who we are. The path then becomes a celebration of freedom lived, cultivated, and protected with the silent devotion of one who knows that the light, once awakened, deserves to be honored at every step.

Chapter 30
Self-Transformation

The journey through the shadows of the past, illuminated by the flame of awareness and propelled by the decision to be free, finally leads us to a new dawn. The process of understanding, confronting, and releasing old pacts, vows, and oaths is not merely an exercise in energetic cleansing or karmic resolution; it is, at its core, a path of profound self-transformation. As we untie the knots that once bound us and heal the wounds associated with them, we do not simply return to a neutral prior state. We emerge different—more conscious, more integrated, and endowed with a renewed sense of personal and spiritual power. Now, at this point in the journey, we can begin to reap and savor the ripe fruits of this inner metamorphosis.

One of the first and most noticeable changes is a palpable sense of lightness. That invisible weight, that "shadow of the past" that accompanied us like a constant presence, begins to dissipate. We feel lighter in our shoulders, in our hearts, in our souls. There is a sense of inner spaciousness expanding, an energetic freedom of movement that once seemed impossible. Accompanying this lightness often comes a new sense of self-possession. We feel more centered, more grounded in our own being, less susceptible to external influences or automatic reactions from the past. Diffuse anxiety diminishes, giving way to deeper peace and growing serenity regarding our personal history. The past, once a source of pain or limitation, comes to be seen with acceptance—as part of the journey that brought us here, but no longer as a burden that defines our present.

Simultaneously, the repetitive patterns and blocks that once tormented us begin to lose their strength. Vicious cycles in relationships, finances, or career start to break. Situations that once seemed inevitable occur less frequently or intensely, or simply disappear. Emotional blocks that once prevented us from feeling or expressing fully begin to give way, allowing for a more natural flow of emotions. Self-sabotage, born of the inner conflict between present desires and past loyalties, diminishes as the energy of the old pact is released and the psyche realigns with current intentions. The disappearance or weakening of these old chains naturally opens space for new possibilities, new paths that once seemed blocked or unimaginable.

This external transformation directly reflects a deep internal reorganization. As we remove the invisible ties that bound us to obsolete commitments, we reclaim precious fragments of our own personal power and vital energy that had been "hijacked" or stagnant within those old contracts. A true reintegration of the self occurs. Parts of us that were dissociated, repressed, or directed toward fulfilling old promises can now return to the center of our awareness and be harmoniously integrated.

This recovered energy, once used to maintain the limiting structure of the pact, now becomes available for growth, creativity, and the realization of our authentic potential.

It is not uncommon that, after deep work in releasing pacts, long-dormant talents begin to awaken. Abilities or interests abandoned due to vows of renunciation or exclusive dedication to something else may re-emerge with renewed strength. Creativity, once blocked by the rigidity of old commitments, may flourish in unexpected ways. With the dissolution of internal conflicts and greater energetic clarity, many people also experience a stronger connection to their life purpose, sensing a clearer and more meaningful direction for channeling their energies and talents. The mental fog lifts, giving way to greater lucidity and the ability to make decisions aligned with inner truth.

It is essential to recognize that this journey of liberation from pacts has simultaneously been a journey of profound self-knowledge and healing. Each step required the courage to face fears, the willingness to retrieve painful memories, the humility to recognize patterns, and the strength of heart to practice forgiveness. In moving through these stages, we have not only broken external ties but also transformed essential parts of ourselves. We have healed old wounds, integrated shadows, developed compassion for our personal story, and strengthened our connection with our divine essence. Liberation is not only about what we leave behind, but about who we become in the process.

There is great merit in having undertaken this journey, often relying primarily on one's own inner strength, intuition, and spiritual connection. Each victory over an old fear, each tie broken by the force of one's own will, each act of sincere forgiveness strengthens self-confidence in an incomparable way. We learn to trust our capacity to navigate the complex landscapes of the soul, to discern our inner truth, and to access the transformative power that resides within us. Trust in the spirituality that supports us also deepens—not as childish dependence, but as a mature partnership with the forces of light that assist us on our path of evolution.

Inspiring stories abound, testifying to the rebirth potential that this self-transformation offers. People who lived for decades trapped in patterns of loneliness and mistrust, after releasing old vows against love, found healthy and fulfilling relationships. Individuals who struggled lifelong with scarcity, upon breaking vows of poverty, saw their finances blossom in unexpected ways. Artists or professionals who felt blocked and invisible, after dissolving pacts of humility or obscurity, finally found recognition and fulfillment in their work. Or simply, people who carried an inexplicable weight in their soul began living with a lightness and joy they had never imagined possible. These are not fairy tales, but real examples of the liberating power that lies in confronting and transforming the soul's hidden contracts.

In essence, the entire process culminates in profound spiritual and personal empowerment. The narrative shifts radically. We are no longer powerless victims of dark forces from the past, of relentless karma, or of irrevocable mistakes. We become conscious co-creators of our reality, authors of our new story. We acknowledge the past, honor its lessons, but claim our power to choose differently in the present and to build a future aligned with our highest truth.

This new awareness, born from crossing inner territories once unexplored, imprints on our soul a kind of spiritual maturity that cannot be taught in books or borrowed words—it is only attained through the courageous experience of one's own journey. It is as if, after passing through a long dark tunnel, we discover that we carried the light all along, and that the true portal of transformation was always within us. This clarity, this intimacy gained with our own essence, becomes the fertile ground where freer choices, truer relationships, and paths more aligned with the heart sprout. Self-transformation thus reveals itself as a silent rebirth, where there is no fanfare, but rather the serene stillness of one who has found their center.

And from this center, we begin to operate in the world with a different presence. Our actions cease to be automatic reactions to old conditioning and become conscious expressions of the being who now fully inhabits itself. We begin to experience reality more vividly, with senses sharpened for beauty, purpose, and truth. Old relationships may renew or dissolve naturally, making room for more authentic connections. Opportunities begin to flow with greater synchronicity, as if life, now resonating with our new vibration, recognizes us and responds generously. In this state of alignment, we realize that there is no need to control everything: there is a deeper trust in our ability to navigate life's cycles and in the wisdom that guides us.

With this renewed confidence, the journey becomes not only a process of liberation but a continuous celebration of the expanding self. We no longer carry the pacts of the past as chains, but as symbols of the crossings that have shaped us. Self-transformation, then, is not an endpoint, but a conscious state of presence that accompanies each choice. It is living with courage, with truth, and with love—not imprisoned by the wounds that once shaped us, but free to express the light that has been revealed in the process. And thus, we become not only more whole but also more available to touch and inspire the world with the clarity and strength that only an awakened soul can radiate.

Chapter 31
Spiritual Freedom

The self-transformation that blossoms along the journey of releasing old pacts is more than a mere improvement in life circumstances or relief from limiting symptoms. It is the gateway to a fundamentally different state of being—a new way of inhabiting the world and relating to oneself and the universe. After all the work of investigation, confrontation, release, and healing, we are invited to contemplate and savor the essence of this achievement: spiritual freedom. This is not merely defined by the absence of specific chains that once bound us; it is an expansive quality of the soul, an inner atmosphere of lightness, clarity, and autonomy that permeates our entire experience.

Imagine the sensation of walking without carrying an invisible burden on your shoulders, breathing without a constant tightness in your chest, looking toward the future without the foreboding that old ghosts might suddenly appear to collect forgotten debts. Spiritual freedom is this state where the soul feels truly unencumbered, light, free of energetic debts or karmic ties that would restrict it to predetermined paths dictated by the past. It is the reclaimed capacity to follow one's own evolutionary path through conscious choice, guided by the inner compass of intuition and present purpose, no longer coerced by unconscious programming or obsolete obligations rooted in old conditioning.

With the dissolution of the energetic and emotional blockages associated with the pacts, vital energy flows with greater vigor and harmony. There is increased mental clarity, sharper intuition, and an expanded capacity to feel and express authentic emotions. The heart, once perhaps guarded behind walls of fear or sadness, can now open more confidently to love, joy, and genuine connection with others and the beauty of life. It is a return to original wholeness, a reclaiming of the spontaneity and vitality that are our birthright but may have been obscured by layers of limiting commitments accumulated along the way.

One of the deepest joys that emerges with spiritual freedom is the serene realization that the past no longer deterministically dictates the present or the future. The lessons contained in the difficult experiences related to the pacts have largely been understood and integrated. The cycles of repetition have been broken through awareness and choice. The energetic debts have been settled through forgiveness and release. What remains of the past is the wisdom gained, no longer the weight of the burden. With this inner resolution, the doors of destiny—once narrow or blocked by self-imposed limitations—now open wide, revealing a horizon of new opportunities, unexplored potentials, and paths that were previously invisible or inaccessible. There is a genuine sense that everything is possible once again.

However, this newly acquired freedom brings with it an inseparable companion: responsibility. While we were bound by the old pacts, we could, consciously or unconsciously, blame these bonds for our difficulties, failures, or unhappiness. "I can't prosper because of that vow of poverty," "I can't find love because of that old promise." These explanations, while perhaps containing a partial truth, also relieved us in some way of full responsibility for our situation. Now, with the ties broken and the excuses of the past dissolved, we become truly responsible for creating our reality from this point forward. Every choice, every thought, every action in the present becomes a brick in the construction of our future.

This is immensely empowering but demands a high level of consciousness and loving vigilance. Spiritual freedom invites us to exercise our free will wisely, to make decisions aligned not with fears or past obligations, but with our highest values—love, compassion, truth, and service to the greater good. Now, more than ever, each choice is made in full autonomy of the soul, and the quality of our future life will directly depend on the quality and intention behind these free choices. It is a call to live more awake, more intentionally, more aligned with our divine essence.

The sensation may be compared to that of a bird who has spent a long time in a cage and suddenly finds the door open. At first, there may be hesitation, perhaps even fear of the vast unknown sky. But soon comes the irresistible impulse to spread its wings, the ecstatic joy of feeling the wind, the wonder of rediscovering the immensity of the horizon. It is a mixture of enthusiasm and perhaps a bit of vertigo in the face of infinite possibilities and the responsibility of choosing the direction of flight. Spiritual freedom returns us to this state of pure potentiality, of openness to the unknown, with the confidence that we possess the inner capacity to navigate it.

It is essential to affirm that spiritual freedom is not a privilege for a chosen few but an innate right of every conscious being. It is the natural state of the soul, to which we are always being called to return. By undertaking the journey of releasing limiting pacts and vows, reclaiming your autonomy, and healing the wounds of the past, you, dear reader, are not merely improving your personal life; you are aligning yourself with the greater purpose of life itself, which is the free and loving evolution of all creation. Every soul that frees itself contributes to the elevation of collective consciousness.

By living this spiritual freedom authentically, you begin to radiate a new frequency into the world, becoming a healing and inspiring presence wherever you are. There is no longer any need to convince anyone of anything or to prove your transformation: the very vibration you emit speaks for itself. A natural serenity arises from the coherence between your inner being and your external choices. This state is not devoid of challenges, but now you face them with different eyes—not as insurmountable obstacles, but as opportunities to grow, to exercise your sovereignty, to refine your truth. And the more you walk from this center of freedom, the more life responds in resonance, opening paths that were previously unimaginable.

Over time, spiritual freedom becomes not merely a destination reached but a daily practice. It is nourished with each conscious gesture, each healthy boundary you set, each time you choose love over fear. It is present in the silences where you listen to your intuition, in the pauses where you honor your rhythm, in the encounters where your full presence transforms the environment. This freedom is silent yet powerful; discreet yet revolutionary. And within it, you remember, day after day, that you are a sovereign being, capable of living with dignity, joy, and truth, guided by the light of your own soul.

At this point, the journey reaches its maturity. There are no longer secret pacts governing your choices, nor ancient voices shaping your steps. What remains now is you—whole, present, awake. Spiritual freedom is not the end of the path but the beginning of a new cycle, where living becomes a conscious art of soul expression. And with each new dawn, you continue to fly—not because you need to escape something, but because you have finally discovered the joy of being who you are in your fullness.

Chapter 32
The Path Ahead

We have reached the end of a profound journey—a passage through the often shadowy, yet ultimately illuminated landscapes of pacts, vows, and oaths that can shape a lifetime. From the desperate cry that gives them birth to the celebration of reclaimed spiritual freedom, we have explored the complex energetic, karmic, and emotional webs of these commitments. Self-transformation has blossomed, lightness has been rediscovered, and the autonomy of the soul has been reclaimed. But, as with every great journey of discovery, the end of one stage is merely the beginning of another. The release from old ties has opened a vast horizon of possibilities—a new path that stretches before us. Now, the question is no longer how to break free, but how to walk in this freedom, how to sustain this new awareness, and how to continue growing and flourishing from this renewed space.

It is essential to understand that the journey of self-transformation is continuous. Freeing oneself from old oaths was not an isolated event with a definitive endpoint, but rather the removal of significant obstacles that had blocked the natural flow of evolution. The space that has opened must now be cultivated with trust and discernment. It is about learning to live without the old crutches, even if they were painful, and to trust in one's own strength and inner guidance to navigate the inevitable challenges and joys that life brings. Walking this new path requires conscious presence, a willingness to keep learning and adjusting, and the maintenance of the practices that brought us to this point.

To sustain the freedom achieved and to avoid falling back into old patterns or creating new limiting ties, it is advisable to maintain regular practices that keep us connected to ourselves and our spiritual source. Continuing the practice of meditation, even for brief daily moments, helps maintain mental clarity, emotional serenity, and connection to inner wisdom. Prayer, or any sincere form of dialogue with the Divine according to one's beliefs, strengthens the sense of support and guidance. Keeping a journal of spiritual insights—recording perceptions, significant dreams, or synchronicities—can be a valuable tool for tracking progress, noticing subtle nuances, and remaining aware of one's inner journey. The attentive self-observation cultivated throughout this process should continue to serve as an ally, helping to quickly identify any tendency to revert to old patterns of thought or behavior. These practices are not obligations but supportive tools that nurture the flame of consciousness and freedom.

A crucial point on the path ahead is loving caution when making new commitments. Having learned—often through difficult experiences—how we can inadvertently imprison ourselves with words spoken without full awareness, we are now invited to approach any new promise, vow, or pact with a much higher level of discernment. Before solemnly committing to anything or anyone, ask yourself: Am I doing this from a place of clarity, love, and free choice, or from fear, lack, guilt, or external pressure? Is this commitment truly aligned with my deepest values and the purpose of my soul at this moment? What are the possible long-term energetic and karmic implications? Honor the lesson learned about the power of words and use them wisely. This does not mean developing a paralyzing fear of commitment; commitment is essential for building relationships, projects, and a meaningful life. Rather, it means choosing our commitments freely, consciously, and responsibly, without resorting to desperate bargains or oaths made under emotional coercion or external imposition. May each new promise be an act of conscious co-creation, not a potential future chain.

Equally important is cultivating the art of living in the present. Much of the suffering associated with old pacts stemmed from being energetically trapped in the past. Now, freed from these bonds, we have the opportunity to inhabit the here and now more fully. Appreciate the lightness of no longer carrying that invisible burden. Savor the sense of space and possibility that has opened. Be present in your interactions, in your work, in your moments of leisure, without the constant filter of past limitations or fears. Living in the present is the most authentic expression of the freedom attained.

In this present living, cultivate gratitude as a state of being. Gratitude for the freedom achieved, for the strength discovered within yourself, for the spiritual support received. Gratitude for the lessons learned, even the hardest ones. And yes, perhaps even gratitude for the pacts of the past. Acknowledge that, despite all the challenges and limitations they may have brought, they were also powerful catalysts for your awakening and growth. They propelled you on this journey of self-discovery and transformation. Integrating the past with gratitude, rather than rejection, is the final seal of healing and inner peace.

Finally, know that you now possess not only freedom but also the knowledge and tools to maintain it. The understanding of the dynamics of pacts, the ability to recognize their signs, the techniques of release and protection—all these are now part of your personal treasury of wisdom. Use this knowledge for yourself, to remain vigilant and free. And perhaps, one day, in an appropriate and respectful way, you may even share your light and experience to help others who may be silently suffering under the yoke of limiting pacts—not as a savior, but as a beacon that illuminates the path toward others' autonomy.

The path ahead now unfolds as a clearer road, lit by your inner achievements and the light of your expanded consciousness. Each step taken with presence, discernment, and love will be a step toward a fuller, more abundant, more joyful existence deeply aligned with the truth of your spiritual essence.

This new stage requires neither haste nor perfection—only presence. Walking forward is not built on grand isolated feats but through the delicate cultivation of daily choices aligned with the being you have become. Small conscious gestures, words spoken from the heart, moments of inner listening, pauses to feel your body and soul—all of these add up to sustain the fertile ground now opening beneath your feet. By honoring your journey with humility and steadiness, you turn everyday life into a living expression of the freedom you have achieved. And when stumbles occur—as they naturally will—let them serve not as reasons for guilt, but as gentle reminders that the path is ongoing and that awareness is the beacon that can always be rekindled.

Allow yourself to dream again. Now that your soul breathes free from its old ties, perhaps forgotten desires may arise, once-silenced yearnings, or even entirely new dreams aligned with your current truth. Trust this creative impulse. The freedom you have gained is not merely the absence of pain; it is also the presence of a soft, profound, and silent power now pulsing more strongly within you. Use it to manifest a life that reflects your true light, no longer needing masks, compromises that betray your essence, or commitments that do not honor your integrity. Walking forward is, above all, living in wholeness—where every part of you, once fragmented, now acts in harmony.

And thus, step by step, may you continue to build a life grounded in clarity, affection, and spiritual sovereignty. May this new awareness accompany you as a faithful guide and companion, helping you face challenges with wisdom and celebrate joys with gratitude. The path is not already laid—it is created with each choice, each act of courage, each moment in which you honor the freedom you have so earnestly sought. And on this new journey, there are no longer pacts binding you—only sacred commitments to your truth, your light, and the unique beauty of your presence in the world.

Epilogue

There is a moment, at the end of every journey, when silence settles not as an absence, but as a full presence. A silence rich with meaning, like the gentle echo of a bell that continues to vibrate even after the ringing has ceased. Upon reaching this point in your reading, you may realize that you have not arrived at an end, but at a beginning. A new starting point where something essential within you has been touched, awakened, realigned.

You have traversed, page by page, a hidden map—not a map of physical lands, but of subtle territories where invisible forces operate, shaping choices, feelings, and circumstances. You have seen, with the eyes of the soul, that there are ancient commitments woven into your journey—some forgotten, others inherited, many still active. You have discovered that there are promises that were not merely words, but energetic decrees, spoken with such emotional force that they echoed beyond time.

And now, you may be feeling something new: the lightness that is born of recognition. The clarity of knowing that, yes, you can dissolve the threads that bind you to pacts that no longer serve your path. That you are not a prisoner of your own old vows, nor of the vibrational inheritances passed down to you—but a conscious guardian of your spiritual freedom.

This is the great alchemy of consciousness: when you become aware of what limits you, you have already begun the process of liberation.

Throughout the chapters, you were invited to look back—to past lives, to silent ancestries, to oaths forgotten in nights of pain or ecstasy. You were guided to recognize that spoken words are not mere sounds but vibrational seeds. And, more importantly, you were shown that none of these seeds are final. That every pact can be transmuted. That the spiritual universe responds to your call when it is born of truth, humility, and clear intention.

What to do with all this now?

Carry forward the art of listening to yourself with greater presence. Reflect on the words that still echo within you. Ask yourself, with honesty: What pacts are still active within me? What promises do I continue to honor unconsciously, even when they no longer make sense? What have I vowed—to life, to others, to myself—that is still shaping my steps?

The answers to these questions will not always come as clear thoughts. Sometimes they will come as a strange sensation when repeating a pattern. Other times, as discomfort before a choice. Or as an unexpected tear when recalling an old scene. Learn to recognize these clues. They are whispers of the soul indicating where the bond still lies.

And when you identify an old vow, do not deny it in anger. Honor the version of yourself who made it.

Embrace that moment with compassion. That pact, however limiting it may have become, was born of a need, a pain, a deep love, or a sincere quest for belonging. It was part of your construction. And now, it can be part of your liberation.

Use the tools this book has offered you—the rituals, symbolic gestures, visualizations, forgiveness, and reconnection exercises. But above all, use your presence. There is no ritual more powerful than being fully present within yourself. And there is no truer liberation than the loving understanding that you are, in essence, free.

You have learned that there are contracts not sealed by spoken words but by persistent thoughts, repeated patterns, silent loyalties. That there are pacts with ideas, with family expectations, with archetypes, and even with former versions of yourself. But you have also seen that every contract, no matter how ancient, can be revoked. For no pact is greater than the truth of your expanding spirit.

And perhaps most importantly: you have understood that your word, when aligned with your heart and soul, has the power to create worlds. It can imprison—but it can also liberate. It can wound—but it can also heal. And now that you know this, choose with awareness what you commit to. Value the word you give. Use it as an instrument of creation, of transformation, of love.

Each vow broken, each pact dissolved, each promise redefined represents a step back to your center. With every thread cut, with every shadow integrated, a new space opens within you—a space to be who you truly are, without bonds, without unchosen contracts, without hidden debts. A space where your life can flourish from your highest will.

What begins now is a new stage: the conscious construction of your commitments. The deliberate choosing of bonds that uplift, that nourish, that expand. The alliance with your own soul—a bond without clauses of fear or submission, but founded in freedom, discernment, and light.

This is not the end of the reading. It is the beginning of listening.

The silence that follows the final pages is fertile. Within it, seeds are germinating. Some will bloom as decisions. Others, as subtle releases. And still others, as new vows—not imposed, but chosen.

May this book have been, for you, more than information: may it have been transformation.

And may the next steps of your journey be walked with lightness, truth, and, above all, freedom.

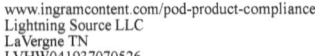
www.ingramcontent.com/pod-product-compliance
Lightning Source LLC
LaVergne TN
LVHW041937070526
838199LV00051BA/2817